easy vegetarian

simple recipes for brunch, lunch and dinner

RYLAND
PETERS
& SMALL

LONDON NEW YORK

Designer Luis Peral-Aranda
Editor Sharon Ashman
Art Director Gabriella Le Grazie
Publishing Director Alison Starling

First published in Great Britain in 2003.

This paperback edition published in 2007
by Ryland Peters & Small
20–21 Jockey's Fields
London WC1R 4BW
www.rylandpeters.com

10 9 8 7

Text © Tessa Bramley, Ursula Ferrigno, Alastair Hendy,
Louise Pickford, Fiona Smith, Fran Warde, Lesley
Waters and Ryland Peters & Small 2003, 2007
Design and photographs
© Ryland Peters & Small 2003, 2007

Printed in China

ISBN: 978 1 84597 492 3

A catalogue record for this book is available from
the British Library.

 For digital editions visit
rylandpeters.com/apps.php

Notes

All spoon measurements are level
unless otherwise specified.

Ovens should be preheated to the
specified temperature. If using a
fan-assisted oven, cooking times
should be reduced according to
the manufacturer's instructions.

Uncooked or partly cooked eggs
should not be served to the very
young, the very old or frail, or to
pregnant women.

Specialist Asian ingredients are
available in larger supermarkets and
Asian stores.

To sterilize preserving jars, wash
them in hot, soapy water and rinse
in boiling water. Place in a large
saucepan and then cover with hot
water. With the saucepan lid on,
bring the water to the boil and
continue boiling for 15 minutes. Turn
off the heat, then leave the jars in
the hot water until just before they
are to be filled. Sterilize the lids for
5 minutes, by boiling, or according
to the manufacturer's instructions.
Jars should be filled and sealed
while they are still hot.

contents

easy peasy

Vegetarian food has become ever-more popular, and not just with those who have chosen to follow a completely meat-free diet. More and more of us are choosing to cut down on the amount of meat we eat and turning to more healthy vegetarian alternatives. But the popularity of vegetarian food is not just down to its healthy reputation. Modern vegetarian cooking has become increasingly delicious and inventive, belying its reputation a decade or so ago as dull, brown and stodgy.

However, if you aren't a seasoned vegetarian cook then it can be daunting to cook without meat. Vegetarian food is often deemed to be time-consuming and difficult to prepare with the misconception that you need to soak and boil pulses for hours on end or spend an eternity peeling and chopping vegetables. This book will dispel that myth. It has easy-to-follow recipes for everything from warming comfort food to fresh and invigorating salads and from quick snacks to more glamorous ideas to serve at a dinner party.

So whether you are a dedicated vegetarian yourself, are looking for menu ideas to cook for your vegetarian friends, or simply want to eat more healthily, this is the book for you.

brunch

400 ml full-fat milk

½ teaspoon ground cinnamon

2 tablespoons clear honey

GRANOLA

200 g rolled oats

50 g oatmeal

50 g oat bran

150 g mixed chopped nuts,
such as hazelnuts, almonds,
macadamias and cashews

2 tablespoons sunflower seeds

2 tablespoons pumpkin seeds

2 tablespoons sesame seeds

50 g raisins

100 g mixed dried fruit,
chopped, such as apricots,
figs, dates, banana and mango

TO SERVE

200 g fresh fruit and berries

extra milk

SERVES 4

This is so yummy – a gooey, sweet, fruity porridge made with a delicious granola mix, soaked overnight in cinnamon-infused milk. Add whatever berries or soft fruits take your fancy just before serving. If there is any granola left over, store it in an airtight container.

cinnamon-soaked granola
with fresh fruits

To make the granola, put the oats into a dry frying pan over medium heat and toast, stirring, until golden brown. Repeat with the oatmeal, oat bran, nuts and seeds, in separate batches. Let cool, then put all the toasted ingredients into a bowl. Add the raisins and mixed dried fruit and mix well.

Put the milk, cinnamon and honey in a saucepan. Heat until almost boiling, then remove from the heat.

Put the granola into individual bowls, pour over the hot milk and let cool.

Refrigerate overnight and serve at room temperature, topped with fresh fruit and berries and extra milk.

APPLE BUTTER

500 g cooking apples, such as Bramleys

3 tablespoons soft brown sugar

a pinch of ground cinnamon

1 teaspoon fresh lemon juice

25 g butter

PANCAKES

125 g self-raising flour

1 teaspoon bicarbonate of soda

25 g fine cornmeal

40 g caster sugar

1 egg, beaten

350 ml buttermilk, at room temperature

15 g butter, melted

125 g small blackberries

oil, for greasing

TO SERVE

single cream

extra blackberries

SERVES 6

blackberry buttermilk pancakes
with apple butter

Apples and blackberries are great together, and here a buttery apple sauce tops blackberry-dotted pancakes. You could replace the blackberries with raspberries or blueberries, if you prefer.

To make the apple butter, peel, core and chop the apples. Put in a saucepan with the sugar, cinnamon, lemon juice and 1 tablespoon water. Bring to the boil, cover and simmer over a low heat for 15–20 minutes until softened. Mash with a fork, add the butter and heat through, uncovered, until thickened. Set aside to cool.

To make the pancakes, sift the flour and bicarbonate of soda into a bowl and stir in the cornmeal and sugar. Put the egg, buttermilk and melted butter into a second bowl and beat until mixed. Stir the buttermilk mixture into the dry ingredients to form a smooth, thick batter. Fold in the blackberries.

Heat a heavy-based, non-stick frying pan until hot, brush lightly with oil and pour in a little of the batter to form a small pancake. Cook for 2 minutes until bubbles appear on the surface. Flip and cook for a further 1 minute until cooked through. Keep the cooked pancakes warm in a low oven while cooking the rest.

Serve the pancakes topped with a spoonful of apple butter, a little single cream and extra blackberries.

warm blueberry and almond muffins

200 g plain flour

1½ teaspoons baking powder

1 teaspoon ground mixed spice

50 g ground almonds

175 g sugar

1 egg

300 ml buttermilk

50 g butter, melted

250 g blueberries

15 g almonds, chopped

12-hole muffin tin with paper muffin cases

MAKES 10

Muffins are quick and easy to prepare and make a lovely breakfast or brunch snack, especially when served warm with coffee.

Preheat the oven to 200°C (400°F) Gas 6. Sift the flour, baking powder and mixed spice into a large bowl and stir in the ground almonds and sugar. Put the egg, buttermilk and melted butter into a second bowl and beat well. Stir into the dry ingredients to make a smooth batter.

Fold in the blueberries, then spoon the mixture into 10 of the muffin cases in the muffin tray until each one is three-quarters full. Sprinkle with the chopped almonds and bake in the preheated oven for 18–20 minutes, until risen and golden. Remove from the oven, let cool on a wire rack and serve warm.

There are few things more enjoyable than eating brunch or breakfast outdoors in the summer. This recipe was inspired by a dish discovered at a café in Balmoral, a pretty beachside suburb of Sydney. Breakfast is big in this city, with hundreds of cafés, bistros and bars offering wonderfully light, healthy food to people *en route* to work. You could replace a handful of the blueberries with raspberries if you like.

berries with honeyed yoghurt

200 g fresh blueberries

a strip of lemon zest

a squeeze of lemon juice

a pinch of ground cinnamon

600 ml plain yoghurt
(not low-fat)

6 tablespoons clear honey

SERVES 4–6

Reserve a few of the best berries for serving and put the remainder into a saucepan. Add the lemon zest, lemon juice, cinnamon and 1 tablespoon water. Heat gently for about 3 minutes until the berries just start to soften slightly. Let cool.

Spoon the berries into individual glasses, then add the yoghurt and honey. Top with the reserved berries and serve.

honey-roasted peaches
with ricotta and coffee bean sugar

Grinding whole coffee beans with lump sugar is typically Italian and adds a delicious crunch to fresh, juicy peaches. This is a mouthwatering recipe, to be enjoyed on a warm summer's morning.

6 large peaches or nectarines

2 tablespoons clear honey

1 tablespoon coffee beans

1 tablespoon lump sugar

300 g chilled ricotta cheese

SERVES 6

Preheat the oven to 220°C (425°F) Gas 7. Cut the peaches or nectarines in half and remove the stones. Line a baking dish with baking parchment and add the peaches or nectarines cut side up. Sprinkle with the honey and roast in the preheated oven for 15–20 minutes, until the fruit is tender and caramelized. Let cool slightly.

Put the coffee beans and sugar into a coffee grinder and work very briefly, until the beans and sugar are coarsely ground.

Spoon the peaches or nectarines onto plates, top with a scoop of ricotta and a sprinkle of the sugary coffee beans, then serve.

french toast and fried tomatoes

Everybody loves French toast. Topping it with fried tomatoes makes a juicy brunch snack. Frying tomatoes seems to intensify their flavour and the heat makes them soft and velvety – truly delicious when served on French toast.

4 eggs

4 tablespoons milk

4 slices bread

50 g butter

8 ripe or green tomatoes, halved

sea salt and freshly ground black pepper

SERVES 4

Beat the eggs, milk and some salt and pepper in a large, shallow dish. Add the bread and let soak for 5 minutes on each side so that all the egg mixture is absorbed.

Heat a large, non-stick frying pan over medium heat. Add the soaked bread and cook over a medium-low heat for 3–4 minutes on each side.

In a separate frying pan, melt the butter. Add the tomatoes and fry for 2 minutes on each side. Put the hot French toast on warmed plates and serve topped with the fried tomatoes.

omelette *fines herbes*

As omelettes are best eaten as soon as they come out of
the pan, I tend to serve this for no more than two people.
However, if you want to make this for larger numbers,
simply multiply the ingredients accordingly.

6 free range eggs

2 tablespoons
freshly chopped
mixed herbs, such
as chervil, chives,
marjoram, parsley
and tarragon

30 g butter

sea salt and
cracked black
pepper

a few extra chives,
to serve

SERVES 2

Put the eggs in a bowl, add half the herbs and salt and pepper to taste.
Beat well. Melt half the butter in an omelette pan until it stops frothing,
then swirl in half the egg mixture.

Sprinkle with half the remaining herbs. Lightly fork through the mixture
a couple of times so that it cooks evenly across the base.

As soon as it is set on the bottom, but is still a little runny in the middle,
transfer to a warmed plate, folding the omelette in half as you go. Sprinkle
with chives and season with salt and pepper. Serve immediately and
repeat with the remaining ingredients to make the second omelette.

starters
and snacks

Fresh asparagus stir-fried with ginger, orange, soy sauce, cashew nuts and a sprinkling of sesame oil makes a very simple yet sophisticated Asian-style starter to grace the table when dining with friends.

ginger asparagus
with cashews

1 tablespoon sunflower oil

375 g asparagus, halved

2 cm fresh ginger, peeled and cut into fine matchsticks

75 g roasted cashew nuts, chopped

grated zest of 1 orange

1 tablespoon soy sauce

1 tablespoon sesame oil

SERVES 4

Heat the sunflower oil in a wok, add the asparagus and ginger and stir-fry for 4 minutes.

Add the cashews, orange zest, soy sauce and sesame oil and continue cooking for 1 minute. Transfer to warm plates and serve immediately.

pesto-stuffed portobello
mushrooms with roasted vine tomatoes

6 slices fresh white bread, crusts removed and discarded

8 tablespoons fresh pesto

8 large portobello mushrooms, stalks removed

olive oil, for brushing

4 large bunches of cherry tomatoes, on the vine

sea salt and freshly ground black pepper

TO SERVE

salad leaves, such as baby spinach or rocket

4 tablespoons extra virgin olive oil

2 tablespoons balsamic vinegar

a handful of basil leaves

SERVES 8

A great cheat's starter: the pesto is store-bought, the mushrooms make instant containers and the vine tomatoes do their artful bit with almost no prodding or encouragement from you. And the cooking? Just minutes, but it will look like you've slaved for hours.

Preheat the oven to 200°C (400°F) Gas 6. To make the stuffing, put the bread into a food processor and blend to make coarse crumbs. Add the pesto, salt and pepper and blend again briefly. Put the mushrooms into a roasting tin, sprinkle with salt and pepper, then brush liberally all over with olive oil. Fill with the pesto stuffing mixture.

Add the vines of cherry tomatoes to the roasting tin and sprinkle with salt, pepper and more olive oil. Roast in the preheated oven for about 8 minutes, or until the tomatoes begin to burst.

To serve, put small bundles of salad leaves on the serving plates and sprinkle with the olive oil and balsamic vinegar. Add a stuffed mushroom and a share of the tomatoes to each plate, top with a few basil leaves and serve.

These delicious little parcels of spinach and creamy ricotta encased in crisp filo pastry are originally from Morocco, but these days they can be found all around the Mediterranean, with countless variations.

spinach and ricotta filo pastries
with slow-roasted tomatoes

6 tomatoes, halved crossways

350 g baby spinach, washed and dried

150 g filo pastry

50 g butter, melted

250 g fresh ricotta cheese

50 g pine nuts, toasted in a dry frying pan

sea salt and freshly ground black pepper

a baking sheet

SERVES 6

To prepare the slow-roasted tomatoes, preheat the oven to 130°C (250°F) Gas ¾. Put the tomato halves, skin side down, into an oven dish, spacing them well apart. Cook in the preheated oven for 2 hours.

Put the spinach into a large saucepan over medium heat. Cook, stirring, until all the leaves have wilted, about 5 minutes. Transfer to a large colander and let cool, while the excess liquid drips out.

Put a clean tea towel onto a work surface and place a sheet of filo on top. Brush with melted butter and layer 3 more of the sheets on top, brushing each with butter. Put the ricotta, pine nuts, cooled spinach, salt and pepper into a bowl and mix. Spread the mixture over the filo, leaving a 5 cm border all around.

Starting with one long side, roll up the filo into a log shape, using the cloth to help you roll. Lightly twist the ends to enclose. Brush all over with butter, transfer to a baking sheet and cook in a preheated oven at 180°C (350°F) Gas 4 for 30 minutes until golden. Slice and serve with the slow-roasted tomatoes.

ricepaper parcels with dipping soy

12 ricepaper wrappers*

2 carrots, cut into matchsticks

6 spring onions, cut into matchsticks

75 g beansprouts

leaves from a bunch of Thai basil

a bunch of watercress

1 tablespoon toasted sesame seeds

DIPPING SOY

2 tablespoons honey

1 tablespoon soy sauce

1 tablespoon teriyaki sauce

1 red chilli, finely sliced

MAKES 12

These are time-consuming but worth it, so enlist some help when assembling if you can. They can be made in advance then kept chilled, covered with clingfilm and a damp cloth, until needed.

Soak the ricepaper wrappers in several changes of warm water until soft, about 4 minutes.

Gather up little mixed clusters of the carrots, spring onions, beansprouts, basil and watercress and put a cluster in the middle of each of the softened wrappers. Sprinkle with toasted sesame seeds and roll up to enclose the vegetables.

To make the dipping soy, put the honey, soy sauce and teriyaki sauce into a small bowl and mix. Add the chilli and transfer to a small, shallow dish to serve with the parcels.

*Note: Vietnamese dried ricepaper wrappers (*bánh tráng*) are sold in Asian markets. Sold in packages of 50–100, they can be resealed and kept in a cool cupboard.

Fennel is a beautiful vegetable, and very versatile. You can roast it with other vegetables or serve it raw in a salad, finely sliced or chopped. The fennel bulbs come in two shapes – very slim and tall, or plump and round. Guess what: the slim ones are male and the plump ones female!

baked fennel
with shallots and spicy dressing

2 fennel bulbs

4 shallots, chopped

1 teaspoon unrefined caster sugar

3 tablespoons olive oil

1 garlic clove, chopped

3 cm fresh ginger, peeled and chopped

a bunch of spring onions, sliced

1 tablespoon sesame oil

freshly squeezed juice of 1 lemon

½ teaspoon chilli powder

sea salt and freshly ground black pepper

SERVES 8

Preheat the oven to 170°C (325°F) Gas 3. Cut the bases off the fennel bulbs and trim the tops. Cut each bulb lengthways into quarters and cut out the hard core. Put into an ovenproof dish and add the shallots, sugar and 2 tablespoons of the olive oil. Mix well and bake in the preheated oven for 30 minutes.

Put the remaining olive oil into a small saucepan, add the garlic and ginger and cook over very low heat for 10 minutes. Add the spring onions, sesame oil, lemon juice, chilli powder and salt and pepper to taste. Gently bring to a simmer, then pour over the roasted fennel, mix well and serve with all the juices.

stuffed peppers

4 long peppers, halved lengthways, cored and deseeded

200 g mushrooms, chopped

150 g mozzarella cheese, drained and cut into large cubes

2 garlic cloves, chopped

3 tablespoons olive oil

75 g olives, pitted and chopped

½ tablespoon paprika

sea salt and freshly ground black pepper

a baking sheet, lightly oiled

SERVES 4

Long, thin, sweet Romano peppers are best for this dish. However, if they aren't in season, ordinary peppers can be used, though a little extra filling may be needed, as they tend to be larger.

Preheat the oven to 180°C (350°F) Gas 4. Put the pepper halves skin side down onto the oiled baking sheet.

Put the mushrooms, mozzarella, garlic, oil, olives and paprika into a bowl. Add salt and pepper to taste and mix well. Spoon the mixture into the peppers. Cook near the top of the preheated oven for 30 minutes. Serve hot or warm.

Mozzarella made with buffalo milk (called *mozzarella di bufala*) has a much creamier, softer texture than mozzarella made from cows' milk. Its superior quality means that it is more expensive than the cows' milk variety, but it's worth it.

mozzarella cheese
with fennel and new potatoes

200 g new potatoes

1 fennel bulb

1 mozzarella cheese, about 125 g

125 ml olive oil

4 tablespoons balsamic vinegar

sea salt and freshly ground black pepper

SERVES 4

Cook the potatoes in a large saucepan of boiling water until just tender, about 12–14 minutes depending on their size. Drain and let cool. When the potatoes are cold, cut them in half and set aside until needed.

Trim the fennel, then cut into halves or quarters. Cut out and discard the hard central core. Using a sharp knife or a mandoline, slice the fennel very finely and set aside.

Slice the mozzarella into thin rounds.

Arrange the potatoes, fennel and mozzarella in stacks on 4 serving plates, seasoning generously between each layer with salt and pepper.

Sprinkle the stacks with olive oil and balsamic vinegar just before serving.

mozzarella-baked tomatoes

If you can find it, use purple basil, which looks even more spectacular than green. This dish really couldn't be easier, and makes a nice change from roasted tomato halves.

20 ripe tomatoes

2 mozzarella cheeses, about 250 g, drained and cut into 20 pieces

100 ml olive oil

a bunch of basil, torn

sea salt and freshly ground black pepper

a large baking sheet, lightly oiled

MAKES 20

Preheat the oven to 170°C (325°F) Gas 3. Cut a deep cross, to about half way down, in the top of each tomato and stuff a piece of mozzarella into each. Transfer to the oiled baking sheet and sprinkle with salt and pepper.

Cook in the preheated oven for 25 minutes until the tomatoes are beginning to soften and open up. Remove from the oven, sprinkle with oil and top with basil. Serve warm.

Garlic bread is everybody's favourite snack. Baguette is traditional but any bread works. Try farmhouse white, cottage loaf, ciabatta, Danish split, wholemeal, mixed grain or individual rolls and cut them accordingly. For a quick variation, slice the loaf and toast it on one side, then spread the other side with garlic butter and grill.

garlic bread

1 loaf of bread

3 garlic cloves

100 g butter, softened

1 teaspoon salt

a bunch of flat leaf parsley, chopped

freshly ground black pepper

a baking sheet

SERVES 4

Preheat the oven to 180°C (350°F) Gas 4. Cut the bread into slices without cutting the crust all the way through, or cut the loaf in half lengthways.

Crush the whole cloves of garlic with the flat of a large knife, then peel, chop and mash to a purée with the salt.

Mix the garlic purée, butter, parsley and pepper in a bowl, then spread generously onto the cut surfaces of the bread.

Wrap the bread in foil, put on a baking sheet and cook in the preheated oven for 20 minutes. Remove the foil and serve hot.

toasted turkish bread

Harissa paste is a hot blend of chillies and spices available from Asian stores, delicatessens and some supermarkets. It's great to have on hand for firing up all sorts of dishes. Stir it into couscous or mix with yoghurt and serve as a dip.

1 teaspoon harissa paste

a bunch of coriander, chopped

2 tablespoons olive oil

50 g pitted olives, chopped

2 Anaheim red chillies, deseeded and chopped

4 slices small Turkish flatbread, pita bread or small flour tortillas, separated into discs

a baking sheet

SERVES 4

Preheat the oven to 170°C (325°F) Gas 3. Put the harissa, coriander, olive oil, olives and chillies in a small bowl and mix well. Divide the mixture between the pieces of bread, then sandwich the pieces of bread together.

Put on a baking sheet and cook in the preheated oven for 10 minutes. Remove and serve hot.

This is such a simple dish that it makes the perfect snack whatever time of day hunger strikes. It tastes amazing, too.

peppered button mushrooms
on buttery toast

4 tablespoons unsalted butter, plus extra for spreading

500 g button mushrooms

4 thick slices white bread

sea salt and freshly ground black pepper

SERVES 4

Working in batches if necessary, put the butter into a large frying pan, melt over medium heat, add the mushrooms and fry until well browned, about 3 minutes. Don't lower the heat too much, otherwise the mushrooms will release all their delicious juices back into the pan and start to boil, rather than fry. Season the mushrooms with salt and plenty of black pepper.

Toast the bread until golden brown and spread generously with butter. Put the toast onto 4 warmed plates and pile the mushrooms on top. Spoon any remaining pan juices over the top, sprinkle with extra pepper and serve.

courgettes and cheddar on toast

This simple combination tastes like heaven – just make sure that you squeeze the grated courgette well otherwise it will make the toast soggy. Vegetarian Worcestershire sauce can be bought from health food stores.

2 courgettes, grated

200 g mature Cheddar cheese, grated

1 shallot, finely chopped

1 egg, lightly beaten

a dash of Worcestershire sauce

4 slices bread, toasted

sea salt and freshly ground black pepper

a baking sheet

SERVES 4

Put the grated courgettes in a clean, dry tea towel and twist tightly, squeezing out all the excess liquid.

Transfer to a mixing bowl and add the cheese, shallot, egg, Worcestershire sauce, salt and pepper. Stir thoroughly.

Put the toasted bread onto a baking sheet, pile the courgette mixture on top and cook under a preheated grill until golden brown. Serve hot.

pan-grilled bruschetta
with red onion marmalade and goats' cheese

2 ciabatta rolls, halved crossways

4 large handfuls of mixed salad leaves

1 tablespoon extra virgin olive oil, plus extra for serving

125 g soft, mild goats' cheese

salt and freshly ground black pepper

RED ONION MARMALADE

2 tablespoons olive oil

750 g red onions, very thinly sliced

1 bay leaf

1 teaspoon thyme leaves

50 g demerara sugar

3 tablespoons balsamic vinegar

150 ml red wine

grated zest and juice of 1 orange

salt and freshly ground black pepper

SERVES 4

Char-grilled bread is more than just toast – it stays chewy on the inside, has a smoky flavour and lovely stripes from the grill pan.

To make the red onion marmalade, heat the oil in a large saucepan until hot. Add the onions, bay leaf, thyme and salt and pepper to taste. Cover with a lid and cook over low heat, stirring occasionally, for 30 minutes, until the onions are soft and translucent.

Add the sugar, vinegar, red wine and the orange zest and juice. Cook uncovered for a further 1½ hours until no liquid is left and the onions are a dark, rich, red colour. Stir frequently during the last 30 minutes to prevent the onions burning.

Let the mixture cool, then transfer to sterilized jars (see page 4). Any leftover marmalade will keep for several weeks in the refrigerator.

Heat a stove-top grill pan until hot. Add the ciabatta and cook for 1–2 minutes on each side until lightly toasted and charred.

Meanwhile, put the salad leaves in a bowl, add the olive oil and salt and pepper to taste. Toss well.

Spread 1 tablespoon of the red onion marmalade on each half of the toasted ciabatta and put onto serving plates. Add a handful of salad leaves and crumble the goats' cheese on top. Sprinkle with olive oil and lots of black pepper.

hoummus and salad
in turkish flatbread

4 sheets of very thin
Turkish flatbread

175 g hoummus

¼ head iceberg lettuce

2 avocados, halved, pitted
and sliced

freshly squeezed juice of
1 lemon

2 tablespoons olive oil

sea salt and freshly ground
black pepper

SERVES 4

If Turkish flatbread is hard to find, use Mexican wraps instead. Pita bread is another alternative – just toast it lightly, open up the pocket and fill.

Open out the flatbreads and put each one on a piece of greaseproof paper. Spread evenly with the hoummus.

Shred the iceberg lettuce finely and sprinkle it over the hoummus. Arrange the sliced avocado on top, then pour over the lemon juice and olive oil. Season generously with salt and pepper.

With the help of the greaseproof paper, roll up the bread and the filling tightly and shape with your hands into a cylinder, twisting the paper at each end.

Cut the cylinders in half. Eat the wraps within 3 hours of making them for a really good, fresh flavour.

Perfect chips need to be cooked twice, at two different temperatures – first to cook them through, then in hotter oil to make them crisp and golden.

root vegetable chunky chips
with coriander mayo

375 g sweet potatoes, cut into thick chips

375 g potatoes, cut into thick chips

375 g parsnips, cut into thick chips

sunflower oil, for frying

sea salt, to serve

CORIANDER MAYO

a large bunch of coriander, chopped

4 tablespoons mayonnaise

a squeeze of fresh lime juice

sea salt and freshly ground black pepper

SERVES 4

Soak all the vegetable chips in a bowl of cold water for 10 minutes to remove excess starch. Drain and dry well with a clean tea towel.

Meanwhile, put the coriander and mayonnaise into a small food processor, add 1 tablespoon water and process until blended. Add the lime juice and salt and pepper to taste. Mix well.

Half fill a deep-fryer or large saucepan with oil and heat to about 180°C (360°F), or until a cube of bread browns in about 60 seconds. Working in 2–3 batches, plunge the vegetable chips into the oil and cook for 6–8 minutes, until cooked through but not golden. Remove and drain on kitchen paper.

Increase the heat to about 195°C (385°F), or until a cube of bread browns in 20 seconds. Plunge the chips back into the oil and cook for 2–3 minutes until golden.

Remove, drain on kitchen paper and sprinkle with salt. Serve at once with the coriander mayo.

4 large portobello mushrooms,
stalks trimmed

1 tablespoon extra virgin
olive oil

4 large ciabatta rolls

sea salt and cracked
black pepper

mixed salad, to serve

SHALLOT JAM

1 tablespoon extra virgin
olive oil

125 g shallots, thinly sliced

2 tablespoons redcurrant jelly

1 tablespoon red wine vinegar

sea salt and freshly ground
black pepper

GARLIC MAYONNAISE

1 free range egg yolk

1 garlic clove, crushed

1 teaspoon freshly squeezed
lemon juice

a pinch of sea salt

150 ml light olive oil

SERVES 4

mushroom burgers
with shallot jam and garlic mayonnaise

If you have any garlic mayonnaise left over, cover it and put
it in the refrigerator – it will keep for up to three days.

To make the shallot jam, heat the oil in a small frying pan, add the
shallots and cook for 15 minutes over low heat without browning. Add
the redcurrant jelly, vinegar and 1 tablespoon water. Cook for a further
10–15 minutes, until reduced and thickened. Add salt and pepper to taste
and let cool.

To make the mayonnaise, put the egg yolk, garlic, lemon juice and salt in
a bowl and whisk until blended. Gradually whisk in the oil, a little at a time,
until thickened and glossy.

Brush the mushrooms all over with the oil and sprinkle with salt and
pepper. Cook in a non-stick frying pan for 4–5 minutes each side. Cut
the ciabatta rolls in half and toast on a preheated stove-top grill pan. Put
the mushrooms on 4 of the toasted ciabatta halves and top with a dollop
of shallot jam, some mayonnaise and the remaining ciabatta halves. Serve
with a mixed salad.

barbecued artichokes
with chilli lime mayonnaise

Try to find small or baby artichokes for this dish so that they can be cooked straight on the barbecue without any blanching first. Larger ones should be blanched in boiling water for a few minutes, then drained before cooking.

18 small artichokes

1 lemon, halved

2 tablespoons extra virgin olive oil

sea salt and freshly ground black pepper

lime wedges, to serve

CHILLI LIME MAYONNAISE

1 dried chipotle chilli

2 egg yolks

300 ml olive oil

freshly squeezed juice of 1 lime

sea salt

SERVES 6

To make the chilli lime mayonnaise, cover the dried chilli with boiling water and let soak for 30 minutes. Drain and pat dry, then cut in half, scrape out the seeds and discard them.

Finely chop the flesh and put into a food processor. Add the egg yolks and a little salt and blend briefly until frothy. With the blade running, pour the oil slowly through the funnel until the sauce is thick and glossy. Add the lime juice and, if the mayonnaise is too thick, 1 tablespoon warm water. Taste and adjust the seasoning, then cover and set aside.

Trim the stalks from the artichokes and cut off the top 2 cm of the globes. Slice the globes in half lengthways, and cut out the central 'choke' if necessary. Rub the cut surfaces all over with the halved lemon to prevent them discolouring.

Toss the artichokes with the oil and a little salt and pepper. Cook over medium-hot coals for 15–20 minutes, depending on their size, until charred and tender, turning halfway through the cooking time. Serve with the chilli lime mayonnaise and wedges of lime.

soups

pasta e fagioli

This hearty soup of pasta and beans is a classic from the region of Puglia in south-east Italy – the pasta shapes traditionally used are orecchiette, meaning 'little ears'.

2 tablespoons olive oil

1 small onion, finely chopped

2 garlic cloves, finely chopped

1 potato, chopped

2 ripe tomatoes, chopped

1.25 litres Vegetable Stock (page 233)

a sprig of thyme, sage or rosemary

800 g canned cannellini beans, drained

150 g small dried pasta shapes, such as orecchiette

a pinch of crushed dried chillies

salt and freshly ground black pepper

freshly grated Parmesan cheese, to serve

SERVES 4

Heat the oil in a large saucepan, add the onion, garlic and potato and cook for 3–4 minutes, stirring occasionally, until golden. Add the tomatoes to the saucepan and cook for 2–3 minutes until softened.

Add the stock, herbs, beans, pasta, dried chillies, salt and pepper. Bring to the boil, then simmer for about 10 minutes, until the pasta and potatoes are cooked.

Ladle into 4 bowls and serve sprinkled with a little grated Parmesan.

The colour and velvety-smooth flavour of this soup make it a winner with the whole family. Serve with crusty country bread.

butternut and cashew nut soup

4 tablespoons olive oil

50 g butter

1 onion, chopped

1 butternut squash, about 1 kg, peeled, deseeded and coarsely chopped

1 teaspoon medium curry powder

200 ml milk

125 g cashew nuts, chopped

sea salt and freshly ground black pepper

country bread, to serve (optional)

SERVES 4

Heat the olive oil and butter in a large saucepan over medium heat. Add the onion and cook for 5 minutes until softened and translucent.

Add the chopped butternut squash, curry powder, salt and pepper. Stir, then cook for 5 minutes.

Pour in the milk and 500 ml water, then bring the mixture to the boil, lower the heat and simmer for 30 minutes.

Add the cashew nuts, then let cool briefly. Working in batches if necessary, transfer the soup to a blender or food processor and blend until smooth and thick. Alternatively, use a hand-held blender and purée in the saucepan.

Reheat the soup as necessary. Taste and adjust the seasoning to your liking, then serve hot accompanied by country bread, if liked.

green bean and herb broth

4 tablespoons olive oil

1 onion, very thinly sliced

1 garlic clove, chopped

1 litre Vegetable Stock (page 233)

200 g French beans, cut into 2 cm pieces

200 g runner beans, cut into 2 cm pieces

200 g shelled broad beans, peeled

a bunch of chervil, chopped

a bunch of dill, chopped

sea salt and freshly ground black pepper

SERVES 4

This soup is great served on its own – it makes a perfect light meal. If you need a dish that is a little more filling, add some pasta or noodles at the same time as the stock. The vegetables and herbs in this soup need only quick, light cooking to bring out their delicate flavours.

Heat the olive oil in a large saucepan. Add the onion and cook over low heat for 10 minutes without letting it brown. Add the garlic and cook gently for a further 5 minutes.

Pour in the stock and add some salt and pepper. Bring to the boil and simmer for 5 minutes.

Add all the beans to the soup and simmer for 4 minutes, then add the chopped fresh herbs and cook for a further 2 minutes. Serve immediately.

In the cold of the winter, a thick, rich soup is a delight every time – serve it with lots of warm, freshly baked bread and cold butter. The tarragon drizzle transforms this rather homely old-fashioned soup into something stylish and modern!

rich root soup
with green tarragon drizzle

1 tablespoon olive oil

2 onions, chopped

1 garlic clove, chopped

3 celery sticks, chopped

400 g parsnips, chopped

400 g swede, chopped

400 g carrots, chopped

3½ teaspoons good-quality vegetable bouillon powder

sea salt and freshly ground black pepper

GREEN TARRAGON DRIZZLE

a bunch of tarragon, finely chopped

freshly squeezed juice of ½ lemon

4 tablespoons olive oil

SERVES 4

Put the oil into a large saucepan, heat gently, then add the onion, garlic and celery and cook for 5 minutes without browning. Add the parsnip, swede and carrot and cook for 3 minutes. Mix the bouillon powder with 1.5 litres boiling water and add to the vegetables. Add salt and pepper to taste, bring to the boil and simmer for 35 minutes, until the vegetables are tender.

Remove from the heat and let cool slightly. Working in batches if necessary, transfer the soup to a blender or food processor and blend until smooth. Alternatively, use a hand-held blender and blend in the saucepan.

To make the drizzle, put the tarragon into a bowl and add the lemon juice and oil. Using a hand-held blender, blend until smooth. Reheat the soup as necessary. Ladle the hot soup into bowls, add a swirl of tarragon drizzle and serve.

wild mushroom soup
with sour cream and chives

Dried porcini have a gorgeous, intense taste and you only need to add a few to fresh mushrooms to produce a lovely, rich soup. Always rinse porcini well, to remove any grit.

10 g dried porcini mushrooms, rinsed thoroughly

50 g butter

500 g large open mushrooms, sliced

2 garlic cloves, crushed

50 g white bread, crusts removed

150 ml sour cream

a small bunch of chives, chopped

sea salt and freshly ground black pepper

SERVES 4

Put the porcini in a small bowl. Cover with 750 ml boiling water and let soak for 30 minutes.

Meanwhile, put the butter into a large saucepan or wok and heat until melted. Add the sliced mushrooms and cook for about 5 minutes until soft.

Drain the porcini, reserving the soaking liquid. Coarsely chop, then add to the mushrooms in the saucepan or wok. Cook for a further 2 minutes, then add the garlic.

Tear the bread into the pan. Add the reserved porcini soaking liquid and salt and pepper to taste. Bring to the boil, reduce the heat and simmer for 10 minutes.

Working in batches if necessary, transfer the soup to a blender or food processor and blend until almost smooth. Reheat the soup as necessary. Ladle into bowls and top with a spoonful of sour cream. Sprinkle with chives and freshly ground black pepper, then serve.

rich red pepper and bean soup

Canned beans can form the basis of lots of filling, easy-to-make soups, salads and main courses, so keep several cans of each kind in your storecupboard.

2 large red peppers, halved, deseeded and cut into 1 cm slices

3 tablespoons olive oil

1 large onion, finely chopped

150 ml dry white wine

820 g canned butter beans, drained and rinsed

700 ml Vegetable Stock (page 233)

125 g fine green beans

sea salt and freshly ground black pepper

chilli oil or garlic oil, to serve

SERVES 4

Preheat the oven to 200°C (400°F) Gas 6. Put the peppers in a roasting tin, pour over 1 tablespoon olive oil and sprinkle with salt and pepper. Transfer to the preheated oven and roast for 30 minutes.

Heat the remaining oil in a large saucepan. Add the onion and cook over medium heat for 10 minutes, or until softened and translucent.

Add the wine to the onion and boil for 1 minute. Add the butter beans and stock and black pepper to taste. Bring to the boil, reduce the heat and simmer for 15 minutes.

Meanwhile, add the green beans to the peppers in the oven and roast for a further 8–10 minutes.

Transfer the butter bean mixture to a blender or food processor and blend until smooth. Reheat the soup as necessary. Ladle into soup plates or bowls, then top with a spoonful of the roasted peppers and beans. Sprinkle with the chilli or garlic oil and serve.

watercress soup

2 tablespoons olive oil

1 onion, chopped

1 leek, chopped

2 large potatoes, chopped

2 teaspoons plain flour

1.2 litres Vegetable Stock
(page 233)

300 g watercress, stalks
removed and
leaves chopped

a bunch of flat leaf parsley,
chopped

sea salt and freshly ground
black pepper

SERVES 8

Watercress has a fresh crunch that releases a subtle peppery taste – a real palate cleanser. Buy it in bunches, with long stems, an abundance of flawless dark green leaves and a clean fresh smell. Store in the refrigerator, wrapped in damp kitchen paper, for up to 2 days.

Heat the oil in a large saucepan and add the onion, leek and potatoes. Cook for 15 minutes until soft and translucent.

Add the flour, mix well, then add the stock and season with salt and pepper. Heat to simmering and cook for 30 minutes.

Using a hand-held blender, blend until smooth. Add the watercress and parsley and simmer for 5 minutes. Adjust the seasoning if necessary, then serve.

**cheese
and eggs**

½ teaspoon cornflour

250 ml milk

500 g Fontina cheese, chopped

50 g unsalted butter (optional)

4 egg yolks

freshly ground white pepper

1 white truffle (optional) or truffle oil

TO SERVE

steamed spring vegetables such as baby carrots, baby leeks, baby turnips, asparagus, fennel and mangetout, cut into bite-sized pieces if necessary

toast or polenta triangles

a double boiler

SERVES 6

The Italian version of fondue is a speciality of the Valle d'Aosta in the north-west. It is made with Fontina cheese, enriched with egg yolks, then sprinkled decadently with shavings of white truffles from neighbouring Piedmont. If you don't happen to have a truffle to hand, a few drops of truffle oil will add a hint of the prized fragrance.

fonduta

Put the cornflour into a small bowl, add 1 tablespoon milk and stir until dissolved – this is called 'slaking'.

Put the remaining milk into the top section of a double boiler, then add the cheese and slaked cornflour. Put over a saucepan of simmering water and heat, stirring constantly, until the cheese melts. Stir in the butter, if using, and remove from the heat.

Put the egg yolks into a bowl and whisk lightly. Whisk in a few tablespoons of the hot cheese mixture to warm the yolks. Pour this mixture back into the double boiler, stirring vigorously. Return the saucepan to the heat and continue stirring until the mixture thickens.

To serve, ladle the cheese mixture into preheated bowls and sprinkle with freshly ground white pepper and shavings of truffle, if using. Alternatively, sprinkle with a few drops of truffle oil. Serve the bowls surrounded by the prepared vegetables, with toast or polenta triangles for dipping.

roasted red pepper cheese fondue

6 small to medium red peppers

125 ml dry white wine or tomato juice

2 tablespoons olive oil

6 spring onions, finely chopped

3 fresh jalapeño chillies, deseeded and finely chopped

185 ml single cream

110 g cream cheese, cut or broken into small pieces

225 g queso fresco or provolone cheese, crumbled or grated

1 tablespoon plain flour

TO SERVE

roasted pumpkin sprinkled with paprika

soft tortillas or sourdough bread

quince paste (*membrillo*)

a, fondue pot

SERVES 6

Roasted red peppers have a sweet acidity that blends wonderfully with cheese. This fondue is delicious served over roasted pumpkin, but boiled potatoes are also good.

Roast the peppers under a very hot grill or in the flames of a gas burner, until blackened all over. Transfer to a large bowl and cover with clingfilm. Let steam for about 10 minutes, then peel off the skin. Halve the peppers and discard the stalks and seeds. Finely slice and reserve one pepper for serving and put the remainder into a food processor or blender. Add the wine or tomato juice and blend to a coarse purée.

Heat the olive oil in a fondue pot and sauté the spring onions and jalapeño chillies until soft, about 5–7 minutes. Stir in the pepper purée and simmer for 5 minutes. Stir in the cream and heat but do not boil. Remove the pot from the heat.

Add the cream cheese, stir until melted and return to the heat. Put the queso fresco or provolone and flour into a bowl, toss well, then gradually add to the fondue, stirring constantly.

Transfer the fondue pot to its tabletop burner and sprinkle with the reserved sliced pepper. Ladle the pepper cheese over the roasted pumpkin and eat with tortillas or sourdough bread. A few slices of quince paste (or *membrillo* in Spanish) would be an interesting accompaniment.

Vacherin is a wonderfully flavourful cheese, found in two styles. Haut-Doubs from France and Vacherin Mont d'Or from Switzerland are soft and pungent cheeses. Vacherin Fribourgeois, a firmer cheese, is the one used in cooking.

vacherin fondue
with caramelized shallots

2 tablespoons butter or olive oil

300 g shallots, thinly sliced

2 teaspoons light brown sugar

2 tablespoons balsamic or cider vinegar

500 ml dry white wine

300 g Gruyère cheese, grated

1 tablespoon plain flour

300 g Vacherin Fribourgeois cheese, grated

2 tablespoons port (optional)

TO SERVE

bread, such as sourdough or baguette, cubed

a selection of fresh vegetables, for dipping

cherry tomatoes

SERVES 6

Put the butter or oil into a cheese fondue pot or large saucepan and melt over medium heat. Add the shallots, reduce the heat to low and cook for 10 minutes. Stir in the sugar, then the balsamic or cider vinegar and cook for a further 10 minutes. Remove a few shallots and set aside for serving.

Pour in the wine, bring to the boil, then reduce to simmering.

Put the Gruyère and flour into a bowl and toss well. Gradually add the cheese to the simmering fondue mixture, stirring constantly. Stir in the Vacherin Fribourgeois, followed by the port, if using.

Transfer the fondue pot to its tabletop burner, add the reserved shallots, and serve the fondue with cubes of bread and vegetables for dipping. Alternatively, put a few slices of baguette into 6 bowls and ladle the fondue over the top.

creamy eggs
with goats' cheese

12 free range eggs

100 ml single cream

2 tablespoons chopped
fresh marjoram

50 g butter

200 g goats' cheese, chopped

a handful of nasturtium
flowers, torn (optional)

sea salt and cracked
black pepper

4 slices toasted walnut bread,
to serve

SERVES 4

Stirring a little creamy goats' cheese into lightly scrambled eggs transforms a simple dish into a delicious light lunch. The nasturtium flowers are optional, but they do add a delightful flash of colour as well as a delicate peppery flavour.

Beat the eggs in a bowl with the cream, marjoram and a little salt and pepper. Melt the butter in a non-stick saucepan, add the eggs and stir over low heat until the eggs are just beginning to set.

Stir in the goats' cheese and continue to cook briefly, still stirring, until the cheese melts into the eggs. Add the nasturtium flowers, if using, and spoon onto the 4 slices of toast. Serve immediately.

rocket eggs with salsa verde

4 free range eggs

1 teaspoon unsalted butter

50 g wild rocket

sea salt and freshly ground
black pepper

ROCKET SALSA VERDE

50 g wild rocket, chopped

½ bunch chives, chopped

4 tablespoons extra virgin
olive oil

sea salt and freshly ground
black pepper

TO SERVE

125 g mixed salad leaves

25 g walnuts, broken
into pieces

fresh Parmesan cheese
shavings

SERVES 2

An omelette-style dish which is fast to cook, so have the ingredients ready before you start. To serve four people, double the ingredients, but make the eggs in two batches.

To make the rocket salsa verde, put the rocket in a blender or food processor, add the chives, olive oil and 2 tablespoons water. Blend until smooth. Add salt and pepper to taste. Set aside.

Crack the eggs into a small bowl and whisk briefly to break up. Add salt and pepper to taste.

Heat the butter in a wok or frying pan until foaming. Add the rocket and cook, stirring, for about 30 seconds.

Add the eggs and gently swirl around the surface of the wok. Cook until golden brown underneath, but still slightly soft and runny on the top.

Meanwhile, divide the salad leaves between 2 plates and sprinkle with the walnuts. Using 2 wooden spoons, cut the omelette into 4 pieces and put on top of the salad. Top with Parmesan shavings and serve at once with the salsa verde.

With its lovely, earthy flavours, a frittata is an Italian version of the Spanish tortilla or the French omelette. Different ingredients are added depending on the region or the season.

mixed mushroom frittata

3 tablespoons extra virgin olive oil

2 shallots, finely chopped

2 garlic cloves, finely chopped

1 tablespoon chopped fresh thyme leaves

300 g mixed wild and cultivated mushrooms, such as chanterelle, portobello, shiitake and cep

6 eggs

2 tablespoons chopped fresh flat leaf parsley

sea salt and freshly ground black pepper

SERVES 6

Put 2 tablespoons oil into a non-stick frying pan, heat gently, then add the shallots, garlic and thyme. Fry gently for 5 minutes until softened but not browned.

Meanwhile, brush off any dirt from the mushrooms and wipe the caps. Chop or slice coarsely and add to the pan. Fry for 4–5 minutes until just starting to release their juices. Remove from the heat.

Put the eggs into a bowl with the parsley and a little salt and pepper, whisk briefly. Add the mushroom mixture to the eggs and stir. Wipe the frying pan clean.

Heat the remaining tablespoon of oil in the clean frying pan and pour in the egg and mushroom mixture. Cook over medium heat for 8–10 minutes until set on the bottom. Transfer the pan to a preheated grill and cook for 2–3 minutes until the top is set and spotted brown. Let cool and serve at room temperature.

salads
and sides

You can make this salad on a grill pan or barbecue, or by roasting the vegetables in the oven. Take your pick.

asparagus and roasted peppers

3 red peppers

2 red onions

400 g asparagus, trimmed

5 tablespoons olive oil

2 tablespoons balsamic vinegar

sea salt and freshly ground black pepper

50 g Parmesan cheese shavings, to serve (optional)

SERVES 4

Cut the pepper flesh away from the core to make flat pieces. Put the pepper skin-side down on a preheated stove-top grill pan and cook until the skin is blistered and turning black.

Transfer the peppers to a small bowl and cover the bowl with clingfilm – allow to steam for 10 minutes. When cool enough to handle, peel the skin away from the flesh.

Cut the onions into wedges, leaving the root end intact to hold them together. Add to the grill pan and cook for 4 minutes on each side. Add the asparagus to the grill pan and cook for about 3 minutes or until just soft.

Put the peppers in a bowl with the onions, asparagus, olive oil, vinegar, salt and pepper. Toss to coat, then serve warm or at room temperature with shavings of Parmesan, if liked.

Hon shimeji mushrooms grow in clumps like families – tiny babies sprout at the feet of the parents. To keep the silkiness of their satin-like flesh, they need a short flying visit to a hot frying pan. If they are unavailable, use sliced shiitakes or regular mushrooms. Here I have used golden beetroot rather than the regular purple kind.

1 tablespoon caster sugar

1 tablespoon balsamic vinegar

1 tablespoon cider vinegar

5 cm fresh ginger, peeled and finely grated

freshly squeezed juice of ½ lemon

3 tablespoons extra virgin olive oil

1 small red onion, halved and sliced lengthways

4 golden beetroot, cooked and peeled

a bundle of small mushrooms, such as Japanese hon shimeji or shiitake

1 garlic clove, finely chopped

sea salt and freshly ground black pepper

SERVES 4

baby mushroom salad
with golden beetroot and ginger

Put the sugar, balsamic and cider vinegars into a bowl and stir until the sugar dissolves. Take the grated ginger in your hand and squeeze the juice into the bowl. Discard the gratings. Add the lemon juice and 2 tablespoons olive oil and beat well, then add the onion.

Cut the beetroot into small wedges, add to the bowl, sprinkle with salt and pepper and mix. Set aside for at least 30 minutes to allow the beetroot to absorb the flavours of the dressing.

Just before serving, put the remaining 1 tablespoon olive oil into a frying pan, heat well, add the mushrooms and garlic and cook over high heat until seared but not soft. Add to the beetroot and toss in the dressing.

Divide the vegetables and dressing between 4 bowls and serve.

new potato salad
with gazpacho dressing

500 g baby new potatoes, scrubbed but not peeled

GAZPACHO DRESSING

2 large, ripe tomatoes, halved, deseeded and chopped

50 g preserved roasted red peppers (in a jar), chopped

½ small red onion, chopped

1 garlic clove, chopped

3 tablespoons extra virgin olive oil

2 teaspoons red wine vinegar

a pinch of sugar

a bunch of flat leaf parsley, coarsely chopped

sea salt and freshly ground black pepper

SERVES 4

Gazpacho is the famous Spanish chilled soup, made with tomatoes, peppers, onions and garlic. Use the same ingredients to make a fresh dressing for this simple salad of new potatoes. Add the dressing to the potatoes while they are hot, even if you aren't eating them straight away, as this will help the flavours to infuse.

Bring a large saucepan of lightly salted water to the boil, add the potatoes and return to the boil. Reduce the heat and simmer for about 12 minutes or until the potatoes are just tender when pierced with a knife.

Meanwhile, put the dressing ingredients into a large bowl and mix well. Add plenty of salt and freshly ground pepper.

Drain the potatoes thoroughly and tip them into the dressing. Mix well and serve hot or at room temperature.

750 g butternut squash, peeled, deseeded and chopped

1 tablespoon extra virgin olive oil

1 tablespoon chopped fresh thyme leaves

500 g dried penne

350 g feta cheese, chopped

350 g cherry tomatoes, halved

4 tablespoons chopped fresh basil

4 tablespoons pumpkin seeds, toasted in a dry frying pan

sea salt and freshly ground black pepper

DRESSING

150 ml extra virgin olive oil

3 tablespoons tapenade

freshly squeezed juice of 1 lemon

1 teaspoon clear honey

sea salt and freshly ground black pepper

SERVES 6

Ready-made tapenade is available from delicatessens and some large supermarkets. Some delis make their own and these are definitely worth seeking out for this dish.

pasta, squash and feta salad
with olive dressing

Preheat the oven to 200°C (400°F) Gas 6. Put the squash into a bowl or plastic bag, then add the oil, thyme, salt and pepper. Toss well, then arrange in a single layer in a roasting tin. Roast in the preheated oven for about 25 minutes until golden and tender. Let cool.

To make the dressing, put the olive oil, tapenade, lemon juice and honey into a bowl. Whisk well, then add salt and pepper to taste.

Bring a large saucepan of lightly salted water to the boil, add the penne and cook for about 10 minutes until al dente (just cooked but still slightly firm in the middle). Drain well, then immediately stir in 4 tablespoons of the dressing. Let cool.

When cool, put the pasta and squash into a salad bowl, mix gently, then add the feta, halved cherry tomatoes, basil and toasted pumpkin seeds. Just before serving, stir in the remaining dressing.

Wintry, festive sumptuousness, thanks to the deep red of the beetroot and the bright white of the cheese.

beetroot, goats' cheese and pine nut salad
with melba toast

750 g small, unpeeled beetroot, trimmed

12 slices white bread

500 g mixed leaves

200 g crumbly goats' cheese

100 g pine nuts, toasted in a dry frying pan

a bunch of basil

2 garlic cloves, chopped

5 tablespoons olive oil

freshly squeezed juice of 2 lemons

sea salt and freshly ground black pepper

SERVES 12

Preheat the oven to 180°C (350°F) Gas 4. Put the beetroot into a roasting tin and roast in the oven for 45 minutes. Remove from the oven, let cool, then peel and quarter.

Meanwhile, to make the melba toast, toast the slices of bread, then remove the crusts. Using a large, sharp knife, split each piece of toast through the middle, to give 2 whole slices of toast with 1 soft bread side each. Cut in half diagonally, then cook under a preheated grill, soft side up, until golden and curled. Watch the toasts carefully, as they can burn quickly.

Put the mixed leaves onto a big serving dish, add the beetroot, crumble the goats' cheese on top, then sprinkle with pine nuts and torn basil leaves.

Put the garlic, oil and lemon juice into a small bowl or jar. Add salt and pepper, mix well, then pour over the salad. Serve with the melba toast.

2 aubergines, about 20 cm, sliced diagonally into 2 cm slices

4 tablespoons olive oil

grated zest of 1 lemon

2 tablespoons thyme leaves

FETA SALAD

24 black olives, pitted and chopped

1 small red onion, chopped

½ cucumber, chopped

2 tomatoes, about 75 g, chopped

75 g feta cheese, crumbled

a bunch of flat leaf parsley, chopped

3 tablespoons olive oil

1 small garlic clove, crushed

freshly squeezed juice of ½ lemon

sea salt and freshly ground black pepper

SERVES 4

aubergine steaks with feta salad

The feta salad adds a lovely touch of summer freshness to this dish. This can be served as a meal in itself, or as an accompaniment to other barbecued dishes.

Put the aubergine slices, oil, lemon zest and thyme in a bowl. Toss to coat and add black pepper to taste. Set aside.

To make the feta salad, put the olives, onion, cucumber, tomatoes, feta, parsley, oil and garlic in a second bowl and mix gently. Set aside.

Cook the aubergine slices on a preheated barbecue or under a medium grill for about 5 minutes on each side until lightly charred and very soft. Sprinkle the salad with lemon juice, salt and pepper to taste. Divide the aubergine and salad between 4 plates and serve.

4 slices country bread, cubed

4 ripe tomatoes, cut
into wedges

15 cm cucumber, peeled and
cut into chunks

1 red onion, sliced

a bunch of flat leaf parsley,
coarsely chopped

100 g olives, pitted

50 g capers

4 tablespoons olive oil

1½ tablespoons wine vinegar

freshly squeezed juice of
½ lemon

1 teaspoon caster sugar

sea salt and freshly ground
black pepper

SERVES 4

This Tuscan salad, better made with day-old bread, is the perfect way to use up leftovers. It is highly flexible so use whatever ingredients you have to hand – sourdough bread, a little garlic, a bunch of basil.

panzanella

Put the bread cubes in a large bowl with the tomato, cucumber, onion and chopped parsley.

Add the olives, capers, olive oil, vinegar, lemon juice, sugar, salt and pepper, then mix well.

Leave the salad to stand for 1 hour before serving so that the bread soaks up the juices and all the flavours mingle.

summer leaf and herb salad

inner leaves from 2 large
cos lettuces

250 g mixed salad leaves,
such as radicchio, mâche
(lamb's lettuce or corn salad),
mizuna or chicory

a handful of mixed, fresh soft
leaf herbs such as basil,
chives, dill and mint

HONEY LEMON DRESSING

1 garlic clove, crushed

125 ml extra virgin olive oil

1 tablespoon freshly squeezed
lemon juice

1 teaspoon clear honey

1 teaspoon Dijon mustard

sea salt and freshly ground
black pepper

SERVES 4

There are thousands of recipes for simple leaf salads, so what makes one better than the next? I think it's just a matter of taste and this version is one of my favourites.

Put the dressing ingredients into a bowl or small jug and set aside to infuse for at least 1 hour. Just before serving, strain out the garlic.

Wash the salad leaves, spin dry in a salad spinner (or pat dry with kitchen paper) and transfer to a plastic bag. Chill for 30 minutes to make the leaves crisp.

Put the leaves and herbs into a large salad bowl, add a little of the dressing and toss well to coat evenly. Add a little more dressing to taste, then serve.

200 g couscous

100 g shelled broad beans, peeled

100 g shelled peas

100 g sugarsnap peas, trimmed

100 g runner beans, chopped

grated zest and juice of 2 lemons

5 tablespoons olive oil

2 teaspoons Spanish sweet paprika

1 garlic clove, chopped

sea salt

SERVES 4

summer beans and couscous salad

A great fresh summer dish. It's full of fresh flavours and looks bright and colourful.

Put the couscous in a bowl, cover with boiling water, mix well, cover and let stand for 10 minutes until swollen.

Bring a large saucepan of water to the boil, then add the broad beans and cook for 5 minutes. Add the peas, sugarsnap peas and runner beans and cook for a further 3 minutes. Drain and refresh under cold running water until the vegetables are cold (otherwise they will lose their bright fresh colour).

Drain the couscous. Transfer to a large bowl and add the beans and peas, lemon zest and juice, oil, paprika, garlic and salt. Mix well, then serve.

tomato tapenade salad

1 small focaccia loaf, torn into
bite-size pieces

8 large tomatoes, each
chopped into 8 pieces

20 kalamata olives, squashed
and pitted

2 tablespoons baby capers,
rinsed and drained

1 garlic clove, chopped

2 tablespoons extra virgin
olive oil

½ teaspoon salt

a pinch of sugar

freshly ground black pepper

TO SERVE

a bunch of basil leaves, torn

extra virgin olive oil

a baking sheet

SERVES 4

In Provence, a tapenade is a paste of anchovies, capers and olives, but I've used just capers and olives as the basis for this salad. Use the ripest red tomatoes, so there are plenty of lovely juices to soak up with the toasted focaccia.

Preheat the oven to 220°C (425°F) Gas 7. Put the focaccia pieces onto a baking sheet. Put in the preheated oven and bake for 12–15 minutes until golden.

Meanwhile, put the tomatoes into a large bowl. Add the olives, capers, garlic, oil, salt, sugar and black pepper and mix.

Divide the toasted focaccia pieces between 4 large serving plates and top with a large spoonful of the tomato mixture. Sprinkle with basil and oil, then serve.

This is a great summer salad. The combination of beans and fresh mint is very refreshing and clean on the palate. To turn this salad into a main course, add some crumbled feta cheese or sliced hard-boiled eggs.

bean and mint salad

200 g broad beans, shelled and peeled

75 g peas, shelled

75 g dwarf or French beans, trimmed

75 g runner beans, sliced into 5 cm pieces

8 spring onions, trimmed and sliced

a large bunch of mint, chopped

3 tablespoons olive oil

grated zest and juice of 1 lemon

sea salt and freshly ground black pepper

SERVES 4

Cook the broad beans in a large saucepan of boiling water for 5 minutes, then add the peas, dwarf or French beans and runner beans and continue cooking for 3 minutes. Drain, cool quickly under cold running water, then drain thoroughly.

Put the spring onions and mint in a large bowl. Add the beans, then sprinkle with the olive oil, lemon zest and juice, salt and pepper. Toss well and serve.

herby potato rösti

Frying creates the lovely crispy crust that's essential for rösti. They are delicious as an accompaniment or simply served with a green salad.

3 large potatoes, peeled

3–4 large sage leaves

a sprig of thyme, leaves stripped

4 tablespoons olive oil

sea salt and freshly ground black pepper

SERVES 6

Grate the potatoes on the coarse side of a box grater and dry well on kitchen paper. Put the grated potato in a bowl.

Finely chop the sage and thyme leaves, discarding any woody stalks. Add the herbs to the grated potato and mix well.

Using your hands, shape a heaped tablespoonful of the mixture into a ball. Shape 2 more potato balls in the same way.

Heat half the oil in a large frying pan until hot. Add the shaped potato cakes to the pan and flatten with a long-handled turner. Fry for 5 minutes until golden on the base.

Turn the rösti over and lower the heat. Continue to cook for 5–10 minutes until golden and cooked through. Transfer to a very low oven to keep them warm. Repeat with the remaining mixture.

Transfer the rösti to a serving plate, sprinkle with salt and pepper and serve immediately.

This is a flavoursome, yet simple alternative to boiled carrots. Sweet and buttery, it is perfect comfort food.

carrot and spinach
butter mash

400 g carrots, peeled and chopped

75 g butter

300 g spinach, chopped

sea salt and freshly ground black pepper

SERVES 8

Cook the carrots in a saucepan of lightly salted boiling water for 20 minutes, or until tender. Drain well.

Return the carrots to the pan and put over low heat. Steam off the excess water, stirring frequently, for 2 minutes.

Remove the pan from the heat, add the butter, salt and pepper and mash the carrots well. Add the spinach to the mash and stir for 2 minutes, until wilted. Serve immediately.

pizzas, savoury tarts and breads

A robust pizza packed with plenty of Italian flavours. To enjoy this at its best, eat it the moment it comes out of the oven, while the cheese is still bubbling.

charred vegetable polenta pizza

1 courgette, thickly sliced

1 small aubergine, cubed

4 plum tomatoes, halved

8 unpeeled garlic cloves

1 red onion, cut into wedges

a few sprigs of thyme

2 tablespoons olive oil

1 quantity Polenta Pizza Dough (page 226)

flour, for dusting

150 g dolcelatte cheese, chopped

sea salt and freshly ground black pepper

a handful of fresh basil leaves, to serve

a pizza stone or large baking sheet

SERVES 4

Preheat the oven to 220°C (425°F) Gas 7 and put a pizza stone or baking sheet into the oven.

Put the courgette, aubergine, tomatoes, garlic, red onion and thyme in a roasting tin. Add salt and pepper and sprinkle with the oil. Cook for 30 minutes, stirring from time to time, until softened and a little charred. Remove from the oven.

Lower the oven temperature to 200°C (400°F) Gas 6. Roll out the dough on a lightly floured surface to 30 cm diameter and spoon the vegetables over the top.

Carefully transfer the dough to the hot pizza stone or baking sheet and cook for 15 minutes. Remove from the oven and top with the dolcelatte. Return the pizza to the oven and cook for a further 5–10 minutes, until crisp and golden.

Sprinkle with the basil leaves, cut into wedges and serve hot.

This is an impressive little number which always goes down a storm.
The herby, zingy gremolata is wonderful with the creamy melted cheese.

molten cheese and gremolata calzone

2 garlic cloves, crushed

15 g flat leaf parsley, finely chopped

grated zest of 1 lemon

1 tablespoon olive oil

400 g Taleggio, Brie or Camembert cheese

double quantity Pizza Dough (page 226)

flour, for dusting

sea salt and freshly ground black pepper

a pizza stone or large baking sheet

SERVES 6

Preheat the oven to 200°C (400°F) Gas 6 and put a pizza stone or baking sheet into the oven.

To make the gremolata, put the garlic, parsley, lemon zest, oil and salt and pepper in a bowl and mix well.

Divide the dough into 6. Put on a lightly floured surface and roll each piece into an oval about 25 cm long. Cut the cheese into 6 even slices or wedges and put a slice on one half of each dough oval. Spoon the gremolata over the cheese. Dampen the edges of the dough and fold the dough over to enclose the filling. Press the edges together firmly to seal.

Transfer to the hot pizza stone or baking sheet, dust with a little flour and bake for 20–25 minutes, until crisp and golden. Serve hot.

Spinach and egg pizzas are a favourite in pizza restaurants everywhere, and you can easily make them at home. It doesn't matter if the yolk is a bit hard, but make sure it goes onto the pizza whole.

fiorentina

350 g young spinach leaves

1 tablespoon butter

2 garlic cloves, crushed

1 quantity Pizza Dough (page 226)

1–2 tablespoons olive oil

1 quantity Tomato Sauce (pages 228–229)

1 mozzarella cheese, about 125 g, drained and thinly sliced

4 free range eggs

50 g fontina or Gruyère cheese, finely grated

sea salt and freshly ground black pepper

a pizza stone or large baking sheet

SERVES 4

Preheat the oven to 220°C (425°F) Gas 7 and put a pizza stone or baking sheet into the oven.

Wash the spinach thoroughly and put into a large saucepan. Cover with a lid and cook for 2–3 minutes, until the spinach wilts. Drain well and, when the spinach is cool enough to handle, squeeze out any excess water with your hands.

Melt the butter in a frying pan and cook the garlic for 1 minute. Add the drained spinach and cook for a further 3–4 minutes. Add salt and pepper to taste.

Divide the dough into 4. Put on a lightly floured surface and roll out each piece to about 17 cm diameter. Brush with a little oil and spoon over the tomato sauce. Put the spinach on the bases, leaving a space in the middle for the egg. Put the mozzarella on top of the spinach, sprinkle with a little more oil, salt and plenty of black pepper.

Carefully transfer to the hot pizza stone or baking sheet and cook for 10 minutes. Remove from the oven and crack an egg into the middle of each pizza. Top with the fontina or Gruyère and return to the oven for a further 5–10 minutes, until the base is crisp and golden and the eggs have just set. Serve immediately.

What is it about caramelized onions? They smell divine, especially when cooked in butter. These simple onion tarts, topped with creamy goats' cheese, are best served warm, although they are also good cold.

onion, thyme and goats' cheese tarts

40 g butter

500 g onions, thinly sliced

2 garlic cloves, crushed

1 tablespoon chopped fresh thyme leaves

350 g ready-made puff pastry, defrosted if frozen

flour, for dusting

200 g log goats' cheese

sea salt and freshly ground black pepper

a baking sheet

MAKES 8

Preheat the oven to 220°C (425°F) Gas 7.

Put the butter into a frying pan, melt over low heat, then add the onion, garlic and thyme and fry gently for 20–25 minutes, until softened and golden. Season with salt and pepper and allow to cool.

Put the pastry onto a lightly floured surface and roll out to form a rectangle, 20 x 40 cm, trimming the edges. Cut the rectangle in half lengthways and into 4 crossways, making 8 pieces about 10 cm square.

Divide the onion mixture between the squares, spreading it over the top, leaving a thin border around the edges. Cut the cheese into 8 slices and arrange in the centre of each square.

Transfer the pastries to a large baking sheet and bake in the preheated oven for about 12–15 minutes until the pastry has risen and the cheese is golden. Let cool a little, then serve warm.

artichoke and cheese tart

This flexible and remarkably easy tart can be topped with all sorts of vegetables and any of your favourite cheeses – the combinations are limitless, so don't hesitate to experiment.

250 g ready-made puff pastry

5 pieces of roasted peppers in oil, drained and cut into 2 cm strips

450 g artichoke hearts in oil, drained

3 onions, sliced

250 g baby leeks, trimmed

250 g cheese, coarsely grated or crumbled

1 egg yolk, beaten

2 tablespoons extra virgin olive oil

sea salt and freshly ground black pepper

a baking sheet, lightly oiled

SERVES 10

Preheat the oven to 180°C (350°F) Gas 4. Roll out the pastry and place on a damp baking sheet. Prick all over with a fork, then bake in the preheated oven for 20 minutes.

Put the roasted peppers in a large bowl with the artichokes, onions, leeks, cheese, salt and pepper. Mix well.

Remove the cooked pastry from the oven, then brush all over with a little egg yolk.

Spread out the filling evenly on the pastry. Return to the oven and bake for a further 30 minutes.

Serve hot or at room temperature, lightly sprinkled with some extra virgin olive oil.

wild mushroom and potato pasties
with parmesan and truffle oil

2 large baking potatoes, unpeeled

60 g unsalted butter, melted

4 fresh porcini, or 2 handfuls other wild mushrooms or 4 small portobellos, sliced

2 garlic cloves, finely chopped

2 sprigs of thyme or flat leaf parsley, chopped, or 2 teaspoons chopped rosemary leaves

500 g ready-made shortcrust pastry, thawed if frozen

flour, for dusting

1–2 teaspoons truffle oil

a chunk of Parmesan cheese, shaved

1 egg, lightly beaten, to glaze

sea salt and freshly ground black pepper

salad leaves, to serve

a baking sheet, lightly oiled

SERVES 4

This is where a little bottle of truffle oil will give extra mushroom flavour and a bit of glamour. Mushrooms, especially wild ones, are natural partners with butter, cheese, potato and truffle oil.

Preheat the oven to 190°C (375°F) Gas 5. Put the potatoes into a saucepan, cover with cold water, bring to the boil and cook until half-done (test with the point of a knife). Drain. Holding the hot potatoes in a cloth, peel off the skins, then cut into thick slices.

Put half the butter into a frying pan, heat until foaming, add the mushrooms, salt and pepper and fry over high heat until beginning to brown on both sides. Add the garlic and herbs, stir-fry for a few seconds, then remove from the heat and let cool.

Put the pastry onto a floured work surface and roll out to about 3 mm thick. Cut into 2 rectangles. Put the potatoes and mushrooms in layers in the middle of each rectangle, sprinkling each layer with truffle oil, shavings of Parmesan, the remaining melted butter, salt and pepper.

Fold in the long edges of the pastry rectangles to contain the filling and make an overlapping join on top. Turn the parcel over and put onto the greased baking sheet. Make 3 parallel diagonal cuts in the tops, brush with the beaten egg, then bake in the preheated oven for about 30 minutes until golden. Cut the parcels diagonally into triangles and serve with salad leaves.

There is nothing more satisfying to bake, or to eat, than homemade bread. This Italian loaf, here spiked with rosemary and cherry tomatoes, is an ideal accompaniment to an Italian soup, such as the Pasta e Fagioli soup on page 62.

focaccia

450 g strong plain flour, plus extra for dusting

7 g sachet easy-blend dried yeast

125 ml virgin olive oil, plus extra for greasing and brushing

12 cherry tomatoes

leaves from a sprig of rosemary

coarse sea salt

a baking sheet, lightly oiled

SERVES 6

Put the flour and yeast into a food processor. With the motor on low speed, gradually add the oil and 300 ml warm water until the mixture forms a soft dough. Remove to a lightly floured surface and knead for 5 minutes.

Transfer to the prepared baking sheet and, using your hands, spread it evenly to the edges. Brush all over with oil, push the cherry tomatoes and rosemary leaves lightly into the surface of the dough at regular intervals and sprinkle with sea salt.

Cover with a damp, clean tea towel and put in a warm place for 40 minutes until doubled in size.

Preheat the oven to 200°C (400°F) Gas 6 and bake for about 20 minutes, until golden. Serve warm or at room temperature.

sodabread

In the past, country people worked hard and the traditional way to top up their energy levels was with a substantial meal at teatime. Served with a good flavourful Cheddar, this lovely bread provides the perfect boost when hunger strikes.

500 g wholemeal flour

1 teaspoon bicarbonate of soda

1 teaspoon cream of tartar

a pinch of salt

25 g butter, cut into small cubes

300 ml milk

flour, for dusting

a baking sheet, lightly floured

MAKES 1 LOAF

Preheat the oven to 180°C (350°F) Gas 4.

Sift the flour, bicarbonate of soda, cream of tartar and salt into a large bowl. Rub the butter into the flour with your fingertips. Make a well in the centre. Pour in the milk and mix with a round-bladed knife to form a soft dough.

Turn out the dough onto a lightly floured surface and knead until smooth, about 4 minutes. Shape the dough into a round loaf 15 cm diameter and flatten the top slightly. Place on the baking sheet and use a sharp knife to score a cross about 1 cm deep in the top of the dough, making quarters.

Bake in the preheated oven for 35 minutes. Remove from the oven and, protecting your hands with a tea towel, tap the bottom of the loaf with your knuckles – when cooked, it should sound hollow; if it doesn't, bake for a few minutes more.

Serve warm, topped with slices of mature Cheddar cheese or spread with butter and jam.

pasta
and noodles

This dish can be rustled up in a matter of minutes. All you need is fresh broccoli and a few basic ingredients.

broccoli and pine nut pesto

175 g dried pasta, such as penne or fusilli

175 g broccoli, cut into florets

2 tablespoons pine nuts

3 tablespoons olive oil

3 garlic cloves, finely chopped

1 red chilli, deseeded and finely chopped

½ lemon

sea salt and freshly ground black pepper

shavings of Parmesan cheese, to serve

SERVES 2

Bring a large saucepan of water to the boil. Add a good pinch of salt, then the pasta, and cook until al dente, according to the instructions on the packet.

Cook the broccoli in a separate saucepan of lightly salted boiling water for 10–12 minutes until very soft. Meanwhile, heat a dry frying pan until hot, add the pine nuts and cook, turning them frequently, until golden and toasted. Transfer to a plate and set aside.

Heat the olive oil in a small saucepan and add the garlic and chilli. Gently cook for 2–3 minutes until softened. Remove from the heat and set aside.

Drain the broccoli, return it to the pan and mash coarsely with a fork.

Drain the pasta and return it to the warm pan. Add the mashed broccoli, garlic and chilli oil and toasted pine nuts. Mix well, squeeze in a little lemon juice and add salt and pepper to taste.

Divide between 2 serving bowls and top with Parmesan shavings. Sprinkle with pepper and serve.

This isn't an ordinary baked lasagne: rather, it's a regular pasta dish, using lasagne sheets dressed with layers of rosemary-scented porcini under blankets of soft cheese. No baking. You can use other mushrooms instead of porcini, just don't use dried porcini.

autumn lasagne with soft goats' cheese

30 g unsalted butter

1 tablespoon olive oil

4 large fresh porcini, or other wild mushrooms or portobellos, sliced

leaves from a sprig of rosemary

16 sheets lasagne

3 free range egg yolks

3 tablespoons cream

250 g soft, mild goats' cheese or ricotta

shavings of Parmesan cheese

sea salt and freshly ground black pepper

SERVES 4

Put the butter and olive oil into a frying pan and heat until foaming. Add the sliced porcini and rosemary leaves and fry until browned on both sides. Remove from the heat and keep the mushrooms warm.

Bring a large saucepan of salted water to the boil, add the lasagne sheets and cook, stirring gently from time to time to keep the sheets separate, until al dente, according to the instructions on the packet.

Put the egg yolks, cream, salt and pepper in a large heatproof bowl set over a saucepan of simmering water. Beat with a metal whisk until the mixture is heated through, about 4 minutes. Drain the lasagne, draping the sheets around the rim of a colander to stop them sticking together, then add to the bowl of egg mixture and toss carefully. (You have 16 sheets, to allow for breakages.)

To assemble, put a folded sheet of dressed lasagne onto each warmed plate. Add a small spoonful of goats' cheese, some shavings of Parmesan and 2 slices of porcini to each serving. Repeat the layers, then top with a sheet of lasagne and extra shavings of Parmesan. Spoon the remaining eggy cream over the top and serve.

A simplified version of that old-time favourite, macaroni cheese, but with no flour and no risk of lumps.

three cheese baked penne

350 g dried pasta, such as penne

400 g mascarpone cheese

2 tablespoons wholegrain mustard

300 g Fontina cheese, grated

4 tablespoons freshly grated Parmesan cheese

sea salt and freshly ground black pepper

a baking dish, about 30 x 20 cm

SERVES 4

Preheat the oven to 200°C (400°F) Gas 6.

Bring a large saucepan of water to the boil. Add a pinch of salt, then the pasta, and cook until al dente, according to the instructions on the packet.

Drain the pasta well and return it to the warm pan. Add the mascarpone and stir to mix. Add the mustard, Fontina and Parmesan, with salt and pepper to taste. Stir to mix.

Transfer to the baking dish and cook in the preheated oven for 25–30 minutes until golden and bubbling. Serve immediately.

pasta with roasted pumpkin
and sage, lemon and mozzarella butter

Tantalizing pockets of melting garlic butter, flavoured with herbs and cheese, complement the succulent chunks of roast pumpkin. The flavoured butter is also brilliant for making garlic bread – it melts between the slices of bread to a deliciously moist and stretchy filling.

2 tablespoons olive oil

500 g pumpkin or butternut squash

1 teaspoon cumin seeds

1 mozzarella cheese, about 125 g, drained and chopped

50 g butter, softened

2 garlic cloves, crushed

2 teaspoons chopped fresh sage leaves, plus extra whole leaves, to serve

grated zest and juice of 1 lemon

300 g dried pasta, such as fusilli bucati or cavatappi

sea salt and freshly ground black pepper

SERVES 4

Preheat the oven to 200°C (400F°) Gas 6. Put the olive oil into a roasting tin and transfer to the oven for 5 minutes, until hot.

Using a small, sharp knife, peel the pumpkin or butternut squash, remove the seeds and cut the flesh into cubes, about 2 cm.

Add the cumin seeds to the hot oil in the roasting tin, then add the pumpkin or butternut squash and salt and pepper to taste. Toss to coat. Roast in the oven for 30 minutes, turning from time to time until tender and golden brown.

Put the mozzarella, butter, garlic, sage, lemon zest and juice, salt and pepper into a food processor. Blend to a coarse paste. Transfer to a sheet of greaseproof paper and roll into a cylinder. Chill for at least 20 minutes or until firm enough to slice.

Meanwhile, bring a large saucepan of water to the boil. Add a good pinch of salt, then the pasta, and cook until al dente, according to the instructions on the packet.

Drain the pasta and return it to the warm pan. Add the roasted pumpkin or butternut squash. Slice or chop the mozzarella butter and add to the pasta. Toss, divide between 4 bowls or plates, top with sage leaves and serve.

simple spaghetti with capers and olives

375 g dried spaghetti

6 tablespoons virgin olive oil

2 garlic cloves, finely chopped

2 tablespoons capers, drained and rinsed, plus a few caperberries (optional)

12 kalamata olives, pitted and chopped

freshly squeezed juice of ½ lemon

8 tablespoons chopped flat leaf parsley

sea salt and freshly ground black pepper

shavings of Parmesan cheese, to serve (optional)

SERVES 4

Don't be tempted to add oil to the pasta cooking water – it is a myth that it stops pasta sticking – and is a waste of good oil! Just make sure you stir occasionally with a wooden fork or spoon while it is cooking.

Bring a large saucepan of water to the boil. Add a good pinch of salt, then the pasta, and cook until al dente, according to the instructions on the packet.

While the spaghetti is cooking, gently heat the oil in a small saucepan. Add the garlic and cook for 1 minute. Add the capers, caperberries, if using, olives and lemon juice and cook for a further 30 seconds. When the pasta is cooked, drain and return it to the warm pan. Add the caper mixture and parsley and toss well to coat. Add freshly ground black pepper and Parmesan shavings, if using, and serve.

300 g silken tofu

1 sachet instant dashi
stock powder

2 spring onions, cut into thirds

6 tablespoons light soy sauce

3 tablespoons mirin
(sweetened Japanese rice
wine) or dry sherry

1 tablespoon sesame oil

2–3 tablespoons sunflower oil

16 shiitake mushrooms,
stems trimmed

2 tablespoons cornflour,
seasoned with salt

250 g soba noodles, cooked
al dente, according to the
packet instructions

TO SERVE

baby pink or yellow oyster
mushrooms

1 tablespoon sesame seeds,
toasted

SERVES 4

Texture. Flavour. Colour. This Japanese dish has it all. Baby oyster mushrooms are best uncooked to keep their fragile texture, moss-like aroma and subtle colour intact. To toast sesame seeds, put them into a dry frying pan and heat gently until they are golden brown, tossing regularly to stop them scorching.

pink oyster and shiitake mushrooms
with crisp tofu and soba noodles

Cut the tofu into 12 small rectangular blocks. Line a plate with 3 sheets of kitchen paper and put the tofu on top to drain for at least 30 minutes.

Put 1 litre water into a saucepan and bring to the boil. Stir in the dashi powder, then add the spring onions, 3 tablespoons soy sauce and 1 tablespoon mirin or dry sherry. Cover with a lid and simmer while you prepare the remaining ingredients.

Put the sesame oil into a frying pan, add 1 tablespoon sunflower oil and heat gently. Add the shiitake mushrooms and fry until lightly browned all over. Add the remaining soy sauce, mirin or dry sherry and 3 tablespoons of the prepared dashi stock, bring to the boil and reduce until syrupy.

Put 1–2 tablespoons sunflower oil into a frying pan and heat well. Dust the drained blocks of tofu with the seasoned cornflour, add to the pan and shallow fry on all sides until crisp.

Divide the cooked noodles between 4 warmed bowls, pour over the hot stock (this will reheat the noodles), top with the cooked mushrooms, crisp tofu, fresh oyster mushrooms and toasted sesame seeds, then serve.

vegetable noodle stir-fry

125 g thin noodles, such as egg noodles

4 tablespoons vegetable oil

1 garlic clove, chopped

5 cm fresh ginger, finely chopped

1 onion, thinly sliced

1 chilli, finely chopped

2 pak choi, about 250 g, roughly chopped

1 leek, cut into strips

75 g beansprouts

75 g mushrooms, sliced

3 tablespoons soy sauce

freshly squeezed juice of 1 lime

a bunch of coriander, chopped

SERVES 4

When making this dish, prepare all the vegetables in advance, so the stir-fry can be quickly and easily put together. Don't overcook the vegetables – they are better when crunchy and brightly coloured. You can change the vegetables according to what you have available, but always use the onion, garlic, ginger and chilli.

Bring a large saucepan of water to the boil. Add the noodles and cook for 1 minute if fresh or 3 minutes if dried. Drain them thoroughly.

Heat the oil in a wok. Add the garlic, ginger, onion and chilli and cook over medium heat, stirring constantly, until softened.

Add the pak choi, leek, beansprouts and mushrooms to the wok and stir-fry for 2–3 minutes.

Add the soy sauce, lime juice and noodles and mix the vegetables and noodles together. Divide between 4 bowls, top with the chopped coriander and serve immediately.

poached mushrooms with egg noodles

4 portobello mushrooms

4 baby leeks

4 shallots

2 bay leaves

200 g dried egg noodles

2 courgettes, sliced into rounds

100 g baby sweetcorn

100 g flat beans, sliced

100 g spinach, chopped

1 tablespoon soy sauce

sea salt and freshly ground black pepper

SERVES 4

The purity and natural flavours of this noodle dish will make you feel very healthy! You can use tofu instead of mushrooms, if you prefer.

Put the mushrooms into a large saucepan and add the leeks, shallots, bay leaves, salt and pepper. Add enough water to cover and heat until simmering. Cover with a lid and cook for 20 minutes.

Add the noodles, and extra water to cover if necessary. Add the courgettes, sweetcorn, beans, spinach and soy sauce. Simmer for 4 minutes, until the noodles and all the vegetables are cooked. Remove the bay leaves and discard.

Serve the vegetables and noodles in 4 bowls with a ladleful of the cooking juices poured over.

This is the perfect healthy choice when you have a number of mouths to feed – it serves 6 people and takes only a matter of minutes to prepare and cook. Other vegetables can always be added, such as asparagus, baby corn, thin green beans, carrots, mushrooms or water chestnuts, whatever you have to hand.

noodle mountain

150 g dried egg noodles

3 tablespoons vegetable oil

2 garlic cloves, chopped

6 cm fresh ginger, peeled and chopped

2 onions, thinly sliced

2 chillies, finely chopped

½ Chinese cabbage, finely shredded

125 g beansprouts

100 ml soy sauce

freshly squeezed juice of 2 limes

1 bunch of spring onions, chopped

200 g cashew nuts, chopped

SERVES 6

Cook the noodles according to the packet instructions, drain and transfer to a bowl of cold water until needed.

Heat the oil in a wok and add the garlic, ginger, onions and chillies. Cook over medium heat for 5 minutes until softened. Add the cabbage and beansprouts and stir briefly.

Drain the noodles well and add to the wok. Toss with 2 large spoons, then add the soy sauce, lime juice, spring onions and cashew nuts. Mix well and serve immediately.

vegetable couscous

2 tablespoons olive oil
2 onions, cut into wedges
2 shallots, peeled
3 garlic cloves, chopped
1 fresh red chilli, chopped
1 teaspoon paprika
½ teaspoon ground cinnamon
½ teaspoon coriander seeds, crushed
½ teaspoon cumin seeds, crushed
4 cardamom pods, crushed
a large pinch of saffron strands
3 carrots, cut into 2 cm chunks
2 parsnips, cut into 2 cm chunks
½ butternut squash, cut into 2 cm chunks
2 courgettes, thickly sliced
400 g canned cherry tomatoes or whole plum tomatoes
600 ml Vegetable Stock (page 233)
400 g canned chickpeas, rinsed and drained
75 g sultanas
sea salt and freshly ground black pepper
a bunch of coriander, chopped, to serve

PINE NUT COUSCOUS
500 g couscous
75 g pine nuts
50 g butter, melted

SERVES 4

This is especially good for a large gathering of people, young and old. Don't be put off by the long list of ingredients – once in the pot, it looks after itself.

Heat the olive oil in a large saucepan. Add the onions, shallots, garlic and chilli and cook for 2 minutes. Add the paprika, cinnamon, coriander and cumin seeds, cardamom and saffron and cook for a further 3 minutes.

Add the carrots, parsnips, butternut squash and courgettes. Cook for 5 minutes, stirring well to coat the vegetables with the spices.

Add the tomatoes, vegetable stock, chickpeas, sultanas, salt and pepper. Make sure all the vegetables are covered with liquid – if not, add extra stock or water as necessary. Bring to the boil and simmer for 20 minutes.

Pour the couscous into a saucepan and add enough boiling water to cover it by 3 cm. Bring to the boil and simmer the couscous for 3 minutes, stirring frequently. Drain well.

Put the pine nuts in a dry frying pan and cook over medium heat, stirring constantly, until browned. Add to the drained couscous.

Pour the melted butter over the couscous and season with salt and pepper. Fluff up the grains with a fork and transfer to a large serving bowl.

Top the couscous with the cooked vegetable mixture and sprinkle with a generous quantity of chopped fresh coriander. Serve hot.

rice

Wonderful produce from a local market in Umbria was the inspiration for this risotto. Garden-fresh courgettes and fluffy ricotta are essential. Italian delicatessens and large supermarkets sell fresh ricotta.

risotto with courgettes and ricotta

100 g unsalted butter

4 small courgettes, about 200 g, chopped

a handful of fresh mint leaves, torn

a handful of fresh flat leaf parsley, chopped

900 ml Vegetable Stock (page 233)

1 tablespoon olive oil

8 shallots, finely chopped

2 garlic cloves, crushed

275 g risotto rice, such as vialone nano, carnaroli or arborio

1 glass white wine, about 125 ml

100 g fresh ricotta cheese

100 g Parmesan cheese, freshly grated

sea salt and freshly ground black pepper

SERVES 4

Melt half the butter in a frying pan, add the courgettes and cook over medium heat until tender, about 5 minutes. Add the mint and parsley and mix well. Set aside.

Put the stock in a saucepan. Heat until almost boiling, then reduce the heat until barely simmering to keep it hot.

Heat the remaining butter and the oil in a sauté pan or heavy-based casserole over medium heat. Add the shallots and cook for 1–2 minutes, until softened but not browned. Add the garlic and mix well.

Add the rice and stir, using a wooden spoon, until the grains are well coated and glistening, about 1 minute. Pour in the wine and stir continuously until it has been completely absorbed.

Add 1 ladle of hot stock and simmer, stirring until the liquid has been absorbed. Continue to add the stock at intervals and cook as before, until all the liquid has been absorbed and the rice is tender but still firm, about 18–20 minutes.

Add the cooked courgettes, ricotta, Parmesan, salt and pepper. Mix well. Remove from the heat, cover and let rest for 2 minutes.

Spoon into warmed bowls and serve immediately.

rice balls

800 ml Vegetable Stock
(page 233)

50 g unsalted butter

275 g risotto rice, such as
vialone nano, carnaroli
or arborio

1 mozzarella cheese, about
125 g, cut into small cubes

6 shallots, finely chopped

a handful of mixed fresh herbs,
such as parsley, basil and
oregano, chopped

finely grated zest of 1 large
unwaxed orange

6 tablespoons freshly grated
Parmesan cheese

6 tablespoons olive oil

sea salt and freshly ground
black pepper

BREADCRUMB COATING

1 egg, lightly beaten

50 g fresh breadcrumbs

MAKES 8

These cheesy rice balls, known as *supplì al telefono*, are enjoyed throughout Italy. In Sicily they are called *arancini*, meaning little oranges. This is a good way of using risotto to make delicious party food or antipasto. It's fun too.

Put the stock in a saucepan. Heat until almost boiling, then reduce the heat until barely simmering to keep it hot.

Melt the butter in a wide saucepan. Add the rice and stir, using a wooden spoon, until the grains are well coated and glistening, about 1 minute. Add 1 ladle of hot stock and simmer, stirring until it has been absorbed. Continue to add the stock at intervals and cook as before, until all the liquid has been absorbed and the rice is tender but still firm, about 18–20 minutes.

Add the mozzarella, shallots, mixed herbs, orange zest, Parmesan, salt and pepper. Mix well. Remove from the heat and let cool. The rice is easier to handle and shape when it is cold.

Using your hands, shape the flavoured rice into 8 balls. Dip each one into the beaten egg and coat well, then roll them in the breadcrumbs, pressing crumbs onto any uncovered area.

Heat the oil in a frying pan, add the rice balls (in batches, if necessary) and cook until golden on all sides, about 8 minutes. Drain well on kitchen paper. Serve hot or cold.

They say that a risotto should be constantly stirred, but this isn't totally necessary. Time is too short. You need to stir it frequently, but while cooking a risotto you can get on with something else in the kitchen at the same time.

mushroom risotto

1 litre Vegetable Stock (page 233)

50 g dried mushrooms such as chanterelles, morels, shiitakes or porcini

25 g butter

1 tablespoon olive oil

1 garlic clove, chopped

1 onion, finely chopped

300 g risotto rice, such as vialone nano, carnaroli or arborio

75 ml dry white wine or vermouth

75 g Parmesan cheese, grated, plus 65 g extra, shaved or grated, to serve

sea salt and freshly ground black pepper

SERVES 4

Put the stock and dried mushrooms in a saucepan and let soak for 10 minutes. Then slowly heat the stock to simmering point. Strain the mushrooms and return the stock to the saucepan to keep hot.

Melt half the butter with the oil in a large saucepan. Add the garlic and onion and cook over medium heat until softened and translucent. Add the rice and stir until all the grains are coated with butter and oil.

Add 1 ladle of hot stock to the rice and mix well. When the rice has absorbed the liquid, add another ladle of stock and stir well. Repeat with the remaining stock, cooking the risotto for 15–20 minutes until all the liquid has been absorbed. Meanwhile, chop the mushrooms into smaller pieces as necessary.

Add the soaked mushrooms, white wine or vermouth, the remaining butter and the grated Parmesan to the risotto. Season to taste with salt and pepper and mix gently over the heat for 2 minutes. Serve with a separate dish of shaved or grated Parmesan to sprinkle over the top.

crusted golden rice bake

This style of rice is inspired by the method used in Persia – crunchy rice is delicious and makes a sensational change from the white and fluffy rice that we know here.

200 g basmati rice

3 tablespoons olive oil

2 onions, chopped

2 garlic cloves, chopped

150 g ready-to-eat dried apricots, chopped

50 g toasted sliced almonds

1 teaspoon ground turmeric

1 teaspoon crushed cardamom pods

1 tablespoon garam masala

100 g butter, cut into small pieces

sea salt and freshly ground black pepper

an ovenproof frying pan, buttered

SERVES 4

Put the rice in a large bowl, wash it in several changes of cold water, then cover with cold water and let soak for 3 hours.

When ready to cook, bring a large saucepan of water to the boil. Add the rice, stir well, return to a simmer and cook for 5 minutes.

Drain the rice and fill the pan with cold water to stop it cooking any more. When cold, drain well.

Preheat the oven to 180°C (350°F) Gas 4. Heat the olive oil in a saucepan, add the onions and garlic and cook for 5 minutes without letting them brown. Add the apricots, toasted almonds, turmeric, cardamom, garam masala and some salt and pepper and mix well.

Stir the spiced onion into the rice, then transfer it to the prepared frying pan and smooth over the top. Dot with butter and cover tightly with foil.

Cook in the preheated oven for 45 minutes, then remove the foil and cook for a further 15 minutes.

Remove from the oven, cover with a large plate and quickly invert both pan and plate. Remove the pan to reveal the rice with its golden crust.

A great favourite in Northern Italy where pumpkin is eaten all year round, not just in autumn. It is used in endless ways – sweet and savoury – from soups to stews and from pasta fillings to flavoured breads and cakes.

pumpkin risotto

900 ml Vegetable Stock (page 233)

50 g unsalted butter

1 tablespoon olive oil

8 shallots, finely chopped

2 garlic cloves, crushed

275 g risotto rice, such as vialone nano, carnaroli or arborio

1 glass white wine, about 125 ml

400 g pumpkin or butternut squash, peeled, deseeded and cut into 1 cm cubes

a handful of fresh flat leaf parsley, coarsely chopped

100 g Parmesan cheese, freshly grated

sea salt and freshly ground black pepper

SERVES 4

Put the stock in a saucepan. Heat until almost boiling, then reduce the heat until barely simmering to keep it hot.

Heat the butter and oil in a sauté pan or heavy-based casserole over medium heat. Add the shallots and cook for 1–2 minutes, until softened but not browned. Add the garlic and mix well.

Add the rice and stir, using a wooden spoon, until the grains are well coated and glistening, about 1 minute. Pour in the wine and stir until it has been completely absorbed.

Add 1 ladle of hot stock, the pumpkin or butternut squash and parsley. Simmer, stirring until the liquid has been absorbed. Continue to add the stock at intervals and cook as before, until the liquid has been absorbed, the pumpkin is cooked and the rice is tender but firm, about 18–20 minutes. Reserve the last ladle of stock.

Add the reserved stock, Parmesan, salt and pepper. Mix well. Remove from the heat, cover and let rest for 2 minutes.

Spoon into warmed bowls and serve immediately.

This dish is so simple which is probably why it's popular with children as well as grown-ups. It's almost impossible to imagine Italian food without tomatoes – use a full-flavoured variety, firm, red and with a good fruity scent.

tomato risotto

900 ml Vegetable Stock (page 233)

50 g unsalted butter

1 tablespoon olive oil

8 shallots, finely chopped

2 garlic cloves, crushed

275 g risotto rice, such as vialone nano, carnaroli or arborio

½ glass white wine, about 75 ml

8 firm tomatoes, deseeded and coarsely chopped

100 g Parmesan cheese, freshly grated, plus extra to serve

a large handful of fresh basil leaves, torn

sea salt and freshly ground black pepper

SERVES 4

Put the stock in a saucepan. Heat until almost boiling, then reduce the heat until barely simmering to keep it hot.

Heat the butter and oil in a sauté pan or heavy-based casserole over medium heat. Add the shallots and cook for 1–2 minutes, until softened but not browned. Add the garlic and mix well.

Add the rice and stir, using a wooden spoon, until the grains are well coated and glistening, about 1 minute. Pour in the wine and stir until it has been completely absorbed.

Add 1 ladle of hot stock and simmer, stirring until it has been absorbed. Repeat. After 10 minutes, add the tomatoes. Continue to add the stock at intervals and cook as before, for a further 8–10 minutes, until the liquid has been absorbed and the tomatoes and rice are tender but still firm. Reserve the last ladle of stock.

Add the reserved stock, Parmesan, basil, salt and pepper. Mix well. Remove from the heat, cover and let rest for 2 minutes.

Spoon into warmed bowls, sprinkle with some freshly grated Parmesan and serve immediately.

artichoke risotto

4 small or 2 large
globe artichokes

1 lemon, halved

900 ml Vegetable Stock
(page 233)

50 g unsalted butter

1 tablespoon olive oil

8 shallots, finely chopped

1 garlic clove, crushed

275 g risotto rice, such as
vialone nano, carnaroli
or arborio

½ glass white wine,
about 75 ml

100 g Parmesan cheese,
freshly grated, plus extra
to serve

2 tablespoons mascarpone
cheese

a handful of fresh flat leaf
parsley, coarsely chopped

sea salt and freshly ground
black pepper

SERVES 4

Try to buy young artichokes with long, uncut stems. The shorter
the stem, the tougher the artichoke tends to be. Young
artichokes are also less fibrous. Firmly closed artichokes are
an indication of freshness; if the leaves are open they are old.

To prepare the artichokes, pull off the tough outer leaves and cut off the spiky, pointed
top. Remove the stalk and cut each artichoke lengthways into 4 segments if small or
8 segments if large. Cut away the fuzzy, prickly choke. Squeeze the lemon over the
segments to prevent discoloration. Set aside.

Put the stock in a saucepan. Heat until almost boiling, then reduce the heat until barely
simmering to keep it hot.

Heat the butter and oil in a sauté pan or heavy-based casserole over medium heat. Add
the shallots and cook for 1–2 minutes, until softened but not browned. Add the garlic
and artichoke segments and cook for 2–3 minutes.

Add the rice and stir, using a wooden spoon, until the grains are well coated and
glistening, about 1 minute. Pour in the wine and stir continuously until it has been
completely absorbed.

Add 1 ladle of hot stock and simmer, stirring until it has been absorbed. Continue to add
the stock at intervals and cook as before, until the liquid has been absorbed and the rice
is tender but firm, about 18–20 minutes.

Add the Parmesan, mascarpone, parsley, salt and pepper. Mix well. Remove from the
heat, cover and let rest for 2 minutes.

Spoon into warmed bowls and serve topped with grated Parmesan.

beans, lentils and chickpeas

haricot bean and tomato salad

750 g new potatoes, unpeeled

about 800 g canned haricot or cannellini beans, drained and rinsed

500 g ripe tomatoes, quartered

4 spring onions, sliced

a bunch of flat leaf parsley, chopped

4 tablespoons extra virgin olive oil

freshly squeezed juice of 1 lemon

sea salt and freshly ground black pepper

SERVES 8

This is a lovely fresh summer salad and perfect for eating *al fresco*. You could serve it as an accompaniment for a barbecue or on its own with some fresh country bread as a light lunch.

Cook the potatoes in a large saucepan of lightly salted boiling water for about 20 minutes, or until tender when pierced with a knife. Drain. When cool enough to handle, cut into wedges and put into a large bowl.

Add the beans, tomatoes, onions and parsley. Sprinkle with olive oil, lemon juice, salt and pepper. Toss gently and serve.

avocado and chickpea salad

2 eggs

250 g baby spinach

400 g canned chickpeas, rinsed and drained

2 ripe avocados, halved, pitted, peeled and sliced

2 teaspoons sweet Spanish paprika

bread such as ciabatta or focaccia, to serve

CREAMY CHIVE DRESSING

freshly squeezed juice of 1 lemon

3 tablespoons milk

2 tablespoons fromage frais or Greek yoghurt

a bunch of chives, chopped

sea salt and freshly ground black pepper

SERVES 4

This is a fresh, instant meal for lazy evenings. When buying avocados, make sure that they are slightly soft to the touch and blemish-free.

Put the eggs in a small saucepan of water, bring to the boil and cook for 8–9 minutes, until hard-boiled. Drain, cool in cold water, shell, cut into quarters and set aside.

To make the dressing, put the lemon juice in a bowl with the milk, fromage frais or yoghurt and chopped chives. Season generously with salt and pepper and stir until smooth.

Put the spinach, chickpeas, avocados and eggs in a bowl. Sprinkle with the sweet paprika, then spoon over the dressing. Serve with fresh bread.

white and green bean salad

The ingredients for this salad are very flexible: haricot beans or chickpeas could be used in place of the butter beans, and other green beans – such as mangetout, sugar snaps or sliced runner beans – in place of the fine green beans.

3 tablespoons olive oil

1 tablespoon balsamic vinegar

800 g canned butter beans, drained and rinsed

300 g fine green beans, trimmed

100 g pumpkin seeds

sea salt and freshly ground black pepper

SERVES 8

Put the oil and vinegar into a large serving bowl. Stir in the butter beans and set aside.

Cook the green beans in a saucepan of lightly salted boiling water for 3 minutes. Drain, refresh in several changes of cold water until cool, then drain again.

Add the green beans and pumpkin seeds to the serving bowl and stir. Sprinkle with salt and pepper and serve.

Most people don't really know what to do with chickpeas. Using the canned variety, as in this super Mediterranean-style salad, dispenses with the soaking that is needed with dried pulses.

chickpea, tomato and pepper salad

5 plum tomatoes, halved and deseeded

3 large red peppers, halved and deseeded

375 g canned chickpeas, rinsed and drained

a bunch of flat leaf parsley, chopped

sea salt and freshly ground black pepper

extra virgin olive oil, to serve

SERVES 4

Preheat the oven to 190°C (375°F) Gas 5. Lightly oil a roasting tin and add the tomatoes and peppers. Cook in the oven for 20 minutes.

Remove the tin from the oven and transfer the tomatoes and peppers to a bowl. Add the drained chickpeas, then mix in the parsley and seasoning.

Transfer the salad to a serving dish, sprinkle with a little olive oil, then serve at room temperature.

warm mediterranean puy lentil salad

100 g cherry tomatoes

300 g Puy lentils or brown lentils

grated zest and juice of 1 lemon

1 fresh bay leaf

2 garlic cloves, chopped

2 red onions, chopped

75 g pitted garlic olives

a bunch of flat leaf parsley, chopped

4 tablespoons extra virgin olive oil

sea salt and freshly ground black pepper

100 g Parmesan or mozzarella cheese, to serve

a baking sheet, lightly oiled

SERVES 4

This is a salad for all seasons. It is wonderful served warm or cold and is bound to become a regular feature on your table.

Preheat the oven to 130°C (250°F) Gas ¾. Put the cherry tomatoes on the prepared baking sheet and cook in the oven for 40 minutes.

Put the lentils in a saucepan. Add the lemon zest and juice, bay leaf, garlic and enough water to cover. Stir, bring to the boil, then simmer for 40 minutes or until the lentils are soft.

Drain the lentils thoroughly and transfer to a large bowl. Add the cherry tomatoes, red onion, olives, parsley, olive oil, salt and pepper. Toss gently, then serve topped with slices of Parmesan or mozzarella.

curried lentils and spinach

4 tablespoons olive oil

1 onion, chopped

1 garlic clove, chopped

1 teaspoon garam masala

1 teaspoon medium-hot
curry powder

½ teaspoon crushed
cardamom pods

250 g brown lentils

2 tomatoes, skinned
and chopped

175 g spinach, cut into ribbons

freshly squeezed juice of
1 lemon

sea salt and freshly ground
black pepper

SERVES 4

Forget any lentil dishes you may not have enjoyed in the past. This is just so delicious: all the extra flavours bring the lentils to life.

Heat the oil in a medium saucepan, add the onion and cook for 5 minutes. Add the garlic, garam masala, curry powder and cardamom, mix well, then cook for 3 minutes.

Add the brown lentils and 500 ml water, bring to the boil, then reduce the heat and simmer for 20 minutes, stirring frequently. When the lentils are soft, add the tomatoes, spinach, lemon juice, salt and pepper. Stir well and serve hot or just warm.

one-dish meals

roasted pumpkin, red onions, baby potatoes and fennel
with chickpeas in tomato sauce

1 butternut squash or ½ pumpkin, cut into wedges, skin left on and seeds left in

3 red onions, cut into wedges

8 baby new potatoes, halved

2 fennel bulbs, trimmed and cut into wedges

3 tablespoons olive oil

410 g canned chickpeas, drained and rinsed

sea salt and freshly ground black pepper

PARMESAN BISCUITS

275 g Parmesan cheese, grated

TOMATO SAUCE

2 tablespoons olive oil

1 onion, chopped

2 celery sticks, chopped

1 leek, chopped

1 garlic clove, chopped

410 g canned chopped tomatoes

1 tablespoon tomato purée

100 ml red wine

sea salt and freshly ground black pepper

a baking sheet, lined with baking parchment

SERVES 4

An easy dish. The tomato sauce can be made the night before – in fact it actually improves overnight.

Preheat the oven to 200°C (400°F) Gas 6. Put the pumpkin or squash, onion, potato and fennel into a roasting tin. Add the oil and sprinkle with salt and pepper. Toss to coat, then roast in the oven for 45 minutes, checking after 30 minutes that the vegetables are cooking evenly and turning them if needed. Add the chickpeas and roast for a further 5–10 minutes until all the vegetables are browned and tender.

To make the Parmesan biscuits, pile teaspoons of the grated Parmesan onto the lined baking sheet and flatten gently to give equal rounds. Bake in a preheated oven at 190°C (375°F) Gas 5 for 5 minutes. Remove the paper from the baking sheet with the biscuits still on it. Replace with another sheet of paper and repeat with the remaining cheese. Let cool.

To make the tomato sauce, heat the oil in a saucepan. Add the onion, celery, leek and garlic and sauté for 5 minutes until soft. Add the tomatoes, tomato purée and red wine. Simmer gently for 30 minutes, adding a little more red wine if the sauce becomes too thick. Using a hand-held blender, process until smooth. Add salt and pepper to taste. Pour the sauce over the roasted vegetables and serve with the Parmesan biscuits.

4 parsnips

1 butternut squash, peeled and deseeded

4 tablespoons olive oil

1 small onion, finely chopped

1 garlic clove, finely chopped

400 ml canned coconut milk

150 ml double cream

a pinch of sugar

50 g walnut halves

sea salt and freshly ground mixed peppercorns

fresh coriander leaves, to serve

CURRY SPICE MIX

1½ tablespoons cumin seeds

1 tablespoon coriander seeds

1–2 teaspoons caraway seeds

black seeds from 4 green cardamom pods, crushed

2 pieces star anise

½ tablespoon fenugreek seeds

½ teaspoon freshly grated nutmeg

1 tablespoon mild curry powder

1 garlic clove, crushed

olive oil, for binding

SERVES 4

You won't need all of the curry spice mix for this dish and what you don't use can be put into a screw-top jar and refrigerated. It is wonderful added to sauces or marinades.

curried parsnips and squash
with walnuts

Preheat the oven to 180°C (350°F) Gas 4. To make the curry mix, grind the spice seeds and star anise to a powder in a spice mill or coffee grinder. Put in a bowl and add the nutmeg, curry powder and garlic. Mix in enough olive oil to make a paste.

Cut the parsnips and squash into evenly-sized pieces. Heat half the oil in a frying pan, add the vegetables and toss quickly to coat. Season lightly, then transfer to an ovenproof dish.

In the same frying pan, heat the remaining oil and fry the onion and garlic until soft. Add 1 tablespoon of the curried paste and cook to release the aromas. Add the coconut milk and cream. Season lightly and add the sugar. Heat gently, then pour the sauce over the vegetables. Cover with foil and cook for about 45 minutes or until the vegetables are tender.

Remove from the oven and sprinkle with the walnuts. Return to the oven and cook, uncovered, for about 15–20 minutes, until the vegetables are golden and the sauce has caramelized slightly. Serve sprinkled with coriander leaves.

2 yellow peppers

6 tablespoons olive oil

1 long, thin aubergine, cut into thick slices

2 red onions, cut into quarters

2 courgettes, cut diagonally into chunks

12 pink garlic cloves

250 ml red wine

12 ripe plum tomatoes, cut in half lengthways

12 black olives, pitted

2 tablespoons balsamic vinegar

1 tablespoon chopped fresh oregano

2 buffalo mozzarella cheeses, about 150 g each, drained and thickly sliced

sea salt and freshly ground black pepper

crusty country bread, to serve

SERVES 4

Fresh oregano is used throughout the Mediterranean and gives this dish a warm, earthy flavour. If you can't get it, use flat leaf parsley or chives instead. Flowering herbs look so beautiful and taste fantastic too, so when in season, serve the vegetables with a sprinkling of purple oregano petals.

vegetable tian
with mozzarella and oregano

Preheat the oven to 200°C (400°F) Gas 6. Roast the peppers under a hot grill or in the preheated oven for 10 minutes or until the skins are charred and blackened. Put them in a plastic bag, seal and let cool. Peel the peppers (the skin will come off easily), then cut them in half and scrape out the seeds. Cut the flesh into thick strips. Set aside.

Heat the oil in a frying pan, add the aubergine and fry briefly. Remove to a plate. In the same pan, fry the onions, courgettes and garlic until just golden. Remove to a plate.

Add the wine to the frying pan and heat gently, stirring to de-glaze the pan juices.

Put the prepared vegetables and plum tomatoes in a shallow, ovenproof dish. Sprinkle with the olives and pour over the heated wine. Pour over the balsamic vinegar and sprinkle with half the oregano. Season with salt and pepper.

Bake in the preheated oven for 20 minutes. Remove from the oven, dot the top with the mozzarella and cook for a further 10–15 minutes or until the cheese has melted and the vegetables are well roasted.

Sprinkle with the remaining oregano and serve with crusty country bread to mop up the lovely juices.

chickpea and vegetable curry

3 tablespoons vegetable oil

2 garlic cloves, crushed

2 red onions, chopped

4 cm fresh ginger, peeled and finely chopped

1 tablespoon curry powder

2 teaspoons ground coriander

½ teaspoon fenugreek

½ teaspoon crushed dried chillies

410 g canned chopped tomatoes

800 g potatoes, cut into 2.5 cm pieces

1 cauliflower, cut into florets

800 g canned chickpeas, drained and rinsed

500 g spinach, chopped

250 g okra, halved lengthways

TO SERVE

naan bread

pappadams

SERVES 12

This curry is very simple to make and you can change any of the vegetables to suit availability. As with all curries this one can be made in advance and left overnight for the flavours to deepen and intensify. You could serve it with the Crusted Golden Rice Bake on page 167.

Heat the oil in a large saucepan, add the garlic, onion and ginger and cook over low heat for 10 minutes until softened. Add the curry powder, coriander, fenugreek and dried chillies, mix well and cook for a further 4 minutes.

Add the tomatoes and 100 ml water, then add the potatoes, cauliflower and chickpeas. Mix well and simmer for about 15 minutes, stirring frequently.

Add the spinach and okra, mix well and simmer for a further 5 minutes. You may need to add a little extra water at this final stage. Serve with naan bread and pappadams.

potato, sage and apple gratin

1.5 kg waxy potatoes,
thinly sliced

1 onion, finely chopped

leaves from 3–4 sprigs of sage

1 tablespoon unsalted butter

4 Granny Smith apples, peeled
and thickly sliced

250 ml double cream

1 egg

a large pinch of freshly
grated nutmeg

sea salt and freshly ground
black pepper

1.5 litre gratin dish, greased

SERVES 4 AS A MAIN DISH

Preheat the oven to 190°C (375°F) Gas 5. Add the potatoes to a saucepan of lightly salted boiling water and cook for 5 minutes. Drain and let cool for a few minutes.

Put a layer of potatoes in the gratin dish and top with a layer of chopped onions. Add a few sage leaves, salt and pepper. Repeat, finishing with a layer of potato.

Melt the butter in a frying pan, add the apples and turn to coat well. Arrange the apples on top of the potatoes, slightly overlapping each slice. Beat the cream and egg until mixed, then add the nutmeg, salt and pepper and mix again. Pour over the apples.

Bake in the preheated oven for about 50 minutes to 1 hour until the potatoes are tender – test by piercing the centre with a skewer. Remove from the oven.

For a golden, nutty top, flash-cook the gratin under a hot grill or use a cook's blowtorch.

Perfect for the busy cook, the vegetables can be layered ahead of time, then topped with the apples before baking. The gratin is delicious on its own or served with vegetarian sausages.

Teriyaki is a Japanese glaze made from sake or mirin (rice wines), shoyu (Japanese soy sauce) and sugar. It is available from large supermarkets or Asian food stores.

honey teriyaki vegetables

2 teaspoons sunflower oil

a bunch of radishes, trimmed and halved lengthways

4 carrots, sliced diagonally

a bunch of spring onions, halved crossways

125 g mangetout, halved lengthways

1 tablespoon sesame seeds, toasted, to serve

DRESSING

1 tablespoon runny honey

2 tablespoons teriyaki sauce

freshly ground black pepper

SERVES 4

To make the dressing, put the honey and teriyaki sauce in a small bowl and mix. Add black pepper to taste.

Put the oil in a wok and heat until hot. Add the vegetables and 2 tablespoons water and stir-fry for about 3 minutes, until the vegetables are just heated through but are still crisp. Transfer to a warm serving dish.

Reduce the heat, add the dressing to the wok and heat it through gently until just warm. Pour the dressing over the vegetables, sprinkle with the sesame seeds and serve.

Chickpeas add a nutty flavour and buttery texture. Sautéing the vegetables first will caramelize their natural sugars to give extra flavour. Serve with crusty bread.

braised root vegetables
with chickpeas and thyme

1 celeriac, about 500 g

3 carrots

4 leeks

2 parsnips

12 shallots

50 g unsalted butter

2 teaspoons brown sugar

400 g canned chickpeas, rinsed and drained

500 ml Vegetable Stock (page 233)

4–5 sprigs of thyme

1 fresh bay leaf, torn in half

sea salt and freshly ground black pepper

TO SERVE

snipped chives

crusty bread (optional)

SERVES 4

Preheat the oven to 150°C (300°F) Gas 2. Peel and trim the vegetables, then cut into bite-sized chunks, but leave the shallots whole.

Heat the butter in a large frying pan, add the vegetables and cook, stirring over high heat until lightly browned. Season with salt and pepper. Sprinkle with the sugar and cook until the vegetables are slightly caramelized. Pour the vegetables into a casserole and add the chickpeas.

Add the stock, thyme and bay leaf to the frying pan and bring to the boil. Pour into the casserole, cover, and cook in the preheated oven for 1 hour. Increase the oven temperature to 200°C (400°F) Gas 6 and cook, uncovered, for about 15–20 minutes until the vegetables are tender and glazed and the cooking liquid has reduced slightly. Season to taste.

Serve sprinkled with chives and accompanied with crusty bread, if liked.

2 tablespoons olive oil

1 large onion, chopped

1 heaped teaspoon brown sugar

3 garlic cloves, crushed

5 dried birdseye chillies, soaked in boiling water to cover

3 tablespoons smoked sweet paprika

1 large parsnip, cut into 2 cm cubes

1 large potato, cubed

200 g baby carrots, trimmed and halved lengthways

800 g canned chopped tomatoes

about 300 ml red wine

410 g canned chickpeas, drained and rinsed

freshly ground black pepper

LEMON AND CUMIN CRACKED WHEAT

300 g bulgar wheat

2 tablespoons virgin olive oil

1 unwaxed lemon, finely chopped

3 teaspoons ground cumin

2 garlic cloves, crushed

freshly ground black pepper

TO SERVE

2 tablespoons Greek yoghurt or sour cream

a bunch of mint, chopped

SERVES 4

vegetable goulash
with lemon and cumin cracked wheat

Paprika gives Hungarian goulash its appealing reddish colour and fragrance. Here the smoked variety, often used in Spanish cookery, adds a distinctive, deep flavour.

Heat the oil in a large saucepan. Add the onion, cover with a lid and cook over medium heat for 10–15 minutes until softened. Remove the lid and stir in the sugar. Increase the heat and cook for 5 minutes until golden.

Add the garlic, drained chillies and paprika and cook for 30 seconds. Add all the vegetables, tomatoes and wine with 300 ml water. Bring to the boil, reduce the heat and simmer, uncovered, for 35–40 minutes until the vegetables are just tender, adding a little extra water if they dry out. Add the chickpeas and some black pepper and simmer for a further 5–10 minutes.

To make the lemon and cumin cracked wheat, put the bulgar wheat in a bowl and add boiling water to cover. Leave to swell for 15–20 minutes until soft, then drain through a sieve, pressing out any excess water.

Heat the oil in a large saucepan. Add the lemon and fry for 2 minutes, then add the cumin and garlic and fry briefly for 30 seconds. Add the bulgar wheat and stir-fry for a further 1–2 minutes. Add plenty of black pepper.

Transfer the goulash to serving plates and spoon over the yoghurt or sour cream. Sprinkle with the chopped mint and serve with the lemon and cumin cracked wheat.

puddings

honey and almond panna cotta
with watermelon and rosewater salad

7 g powdered vegetarian gelatin (agar agar)

200 ml double cream

250 g Greek yoghurt

25 g caster sugar

6 tablespoons clear honey

50 g ground almonds

1 vanilla pod, split lengthways and seeds scraped out

WATERMELON AND ROSEWATER SALAD

8–12 unsprayed pink rose petals

1 egg white, beaten

1 tablespoon caster sugar

1 small watermelon, about 1.5 kg, chilled

2 tablespoons rosewater

4 metal or china ramekins, lightly oiled and lined with muslin or clingfilm

SERVES 4

This is a very pretty yet simple pudding. It is the perfect choice if you are entertaining as you can make it in advance. If you don't have individual ramekins, use one large bowl for the panna cotta.

To make the panna cotta, put 3 tablespoons warm water in a small bowl, sprinkle the gelatin evenly over the top and set aside until dissolved, about 5 minutes.

Put the cream in a mixing bowl. Add the yoghurt, sugar and honey and stir until smooth. Mix in the ground almonds, vanilla seeds and gelatin.

Pour the cream mixture into the prepared ramekins, then chill for 4 hours or until set.

Meanwhile, prepare the watermelon and rosewater salad. Dip the rose petals in the beaten egg white, then lightly dust with caster sugar, and set aside to dry for 1 hour.

Top and tail the watermelon, then slice it into thin wedges and remove the seeds. Arrange the slices on a large serving plate, then sprinkle with the rosewater. Cover and chill until needed.

To serve, turn the panna cotta out onto small plates. Accompany with the watermelon slices and decorate with the sugar-dusted rose petals.

Although not, strictly speaking, a crumble, this pudding has a beautifully crisp topping. If you don't particularly like ginger, try finely grated orange zest instead. Both flavours work equally well with rhubarb.

rhubarb crumble
with ginger and vanilla

675 g forced rhubarb, cut into 2 cm pieces

3 pieces of crystallized ginger, cut into matchsticks

115 g caster sugar

1 vanilla pod, split lengthways and seeds scraped out

CRUMBLE TOPPING

85 g flaked almonds

85 g unsalted butter

115 g brown breadcrumbs

55 g rolled oats

55 g brown sugar

4 individual ovenproof dishes, or a shallow baking dish

SERVES 4

Preheat the oven to 200°C (400°F) Gas 6. Put the rhubarb, ginger, caster sugar and vanilla seeds into a saucepan and cook over low heat until the juices run from the rhubarb and it starts to soften. Pour into the ovenproof dishes or baking dish.

To make the topping, put the almonds into a dry frying pan and cook, stirring, over low heat until lightly golden. Take care or they may burn. Remove and reserve.

Add the butter to the frying pan and heat gently until melted. Add the breadcrumbs, rolled oats and brown sugar. Increase the heat and cook briskly, stirring continuously, until the breadcrumbs and oats start to caramelize, brown and separate. Remove from the pan and stir in the toasted almonds.

Sprinkle the mixture over the rhubarb, starting at the edges and working towards the middle. Press down firmly. Transfer to the preheated oven and cook for about 10 minutes until the topping is crisp and golden (the forced rhubarb is very tender and will finish cooking in this time).

nectarine tart

Crumbly sweet pastry and oozingly juicy nectarines make a sensational combination. Come autumn, plums make a lovely alternative filling.

240 g plain flour, plus extra for dusting

250 g butter, softened and cut into small pieces

100 g icing sugar, plus extra for dusting

2–3 egg yolks

1.25 kg nectarines or peaches

real vanilla ice cream, Greek yoghurt and honey or crème fraîche, to serve

a 20 cm loose-based tart tin

SERVES 6–8

Put the flour, butter and icing sugar in a food processor and whizz until the mixture looks like breadcrumbs. Add the egg yolks and blend the mixture again, just until it comes together to form a ball of dough. Wrap the pastry in clingfilm and chill for at least 30 minutes.

Preheat the oven to 190°C (375°F) Gas 5. Knead the pastry briefly to soften, then roll out the pastry on a lightly floured work surface into a large circle at least 5 cm wider than the base of the tart tin.

Drape the pastry over the rolling pin, carefully lift it up and place it over the top of the tin. Gently press the pastry into the tin, making sure there are no air pockets. This pastry is very fragile, but don't despair. Just line your tart tin as best you can, and then patch up any cracks with extra pieces of pastry. Use a sharp knife to trim off the excess pastry. Chill the tart case for 15 minutes.

Cut the nectarines or peaches in half, twist to remove the stone, then cut the fruit into slices. Remove the pastry case from the fridge and, working from the outside, arrange the nectarine or peach slices in circles on the pastry, until all the fruit has been used.

Bake in the preheated oven for 30 minutes, then reduce the heat to 150°C (300°F) Gas 2 and continue cooking for a further 40 minutes until the fruit is tender and golden and the pastry is crisp.

Dust the tart with icing sugar, then serve hot or cold with scoops of good-quality vanilla ice cream, Greek yoghurt sprinkled with honey, or crème fraîche.

Foolproof and very quick to prepare, tiramisu is a wonderful pudding to serve a large group of people – it can be made in advance, doesn't need cooking or heating and tastes so delicious that it is universally welcomed. You can present it in individual glasses or one large serving bowl.

tiramisu

50 amaretti biscuits, crushed

200 ml Kahlúa (coffee liqueur)

6 tablespoons brandy

100 ml strong black coffee

1 kg mascarpone cheese

8 free range eggs separated

100 g caster sugar, sifted

250 g dark chocolate, grated, or 4 tablespoons cocoa powder

20 individual glasses or a large serving dish

SERVES 20

Arrange a quarter of the crushed amaretti biscuits at the bottom of the glasses or serving dish. Mix the Kahlúa in a small bowl with the brandy and coffee and pour a quarter of this mixture over the crushed biscuits in the glasses or serving dish.

Put the mascarpone, egg yolks and caster sugar in a bowl and beat until smooth and lump-free. Put the egg whites in a separate bowl, whisk until stiff, then gently fold them into the mascarpone mixture.

Spoon a quarter of the mixture over the biscuits, then repeat the layers 3 times, finishing with a layer of mascarpone mixture.

Sprinkle the chocolate or cocoa over the top of the tiramisu and refrigerate overnight. Serve chilled or at room temperature.

warm chocolate and coffee pudding

1 teaspoon instant coffee

175 g butter

175 g unrefined caster sugar

2 large eggs

225 g self-raising flour

50 g cocoa powder

milk, as needed

single cream, to serve

CHOCOLATE SAUCE

100 g plain chocolate
(70 per cent cocoa solids),
broken into pieces

100 g butter

50 g unrefined caster sugar

200 ml double cream

a 1 litre pudding basin, buttered

SERVES 8

This pudding can be made in advance, then reheated when required. Don't scrimp on the chocolate sauce ingredients: they make a thick, rich and glossy sauce that will become one of your prized favourites. You can also serve the sauce over poached pears, ice cream or other puddings.

Put the coffee into a small cup, add 1 teaspoon boiling water and stir to dissolve. Put 10 cm water into a saucepan large enough to hold the pudding basin. Put the butter and sugar into a bowl and, using an electric whisk, beat until creamy, light and very pale. Add the eggs and coffee and beat again.

Sift in the flour and cocoa powder and fold in with a large metal spoon, adding a little milk if the mixture seems very stiff. Transfer to the prepared pudding basin and cover tightly with buttered foil or greaseproof paper. Put the basin into the saucepan of water, cover the saucepan with a lid and bring the water to the boil. Reduce the heat and simmer for 1½ hours, checking the water level from time to time and topping up if necessary.

To make the sauce, put the chocolate, butter, sugar and cream into a small saucepan. Heat gently, stirring frequently, until melted. Remove from the heat and set aside until ready to serve.

Remove the basin from the saucepan and carefully turn out the pudding onto a large plate. Serve hot or warm with the chocolate sauce and single cream.

In this sumptuous dessert, the sweetness of the meringue is offset by the sharpness of the fruit. All sorts of different fruits can be used.

raspberry and passionfruit pavlova

4 large egg whites

a pinch of salt

375 g caster sugar

1 tablespoon sugar

1 tablespoon cornflour

2 teaspoons freshly squeezed lemon juice

sprigs of mint, to decorate (optional)

FILLING

300 ml double cream, whipped

300 g raspberries

3–4 passionfruit

RASPBERRY PURÉE (OPTIONAL)

300 g raspberries

1–2 tablespoons icing sugar, sifted

a baking sheet, lined with baking parchment and sprinkled with cornflour

SERVES 6–8

Preheat the oven to 120°C (240°F) Gas ½. Put the egg whites and salt into a large bowl and, using an electric mixer, whisk the egg whites until stiff. Gradually add two-thirds of the caster sugar, whisking between each addition until the meringue is very glossy and stiff. Whisk in the remaining caster sugar.

Sift the sugar and cornflour together into a small bowl and mix well. Fold half the cornflour mixture into the meringue, then 1 teaspoon of the lemon juice. Repeat with the remaining cornflour mixture and lemon juice.

Spoon half the meringue onto the baking parchment and spread out to a disc about 18 cm diameter. Smooth the top and sides. Spoon the rest of the meringue in a ring around the edge of the disc until the pavlova is about 6 cm thick at the edges.

Bake in the preheated oven for about 1–1¼ hours. Remove from the oven and let cool. Alternatively, switch off the oven and leave the meringue inside until cool. This will help reduce cracking.

To make the raspberry purée, crush the raspberries with a fork or hand-held stick blender, then press through a sieve to make a purée. Discard the seeds. Mix in enough of the icing sugar to sweeten to taste.

When the pavlova is cold, carefully remove the baking parchment and put the pavlova onto a serving plate. Fill the centre with the whipped cream and top with the raspberries. Cut the passionfruit in half and scoop out the pulp and seeds onto the raspberries. Serve decorated with a few sprigs of mint and the raspberry purée, if using.

The quintessential nursery pudding – and the definitive comfort food. It's very simple to make and when served like this – with a caramelized sugar top – it is sophisticated enough for even the smartest dinner party.

rice pudding
with caramelized pineapple and banana

25 g unsalted butter

1 tablespoon caster sugar, plus extra for dusting

75 g risotto rice, such as vialone nano, carnaroli or arborio

500 ml milk

250 ml single cream

1 strip of lemon zest

a pinch of salt

1 vanilla pod, split in half lengthways

4 thick slices of fresh pineapple

2 bananas

icing sugar, for dusting

4 large ramekins

8 wooden satay sticks, soaked in water for 20 minutes

SERVES 4

Preheat the oven to 140°C (275°F) Gas 1. Put the butter and sugar into a saucepan and heat until foaming. Stir in the rice, coating the grains until they glisten. In another pan, heat the milk gently until boiling, then gradually add to the rice, stirring frequently. Add the cream, lemon zest and salt.

Scrape the seeds from the vanilla pod into the rice mixture, then add the pod. Heat until almost boiling, then pour into a deep, ovenproof dish. Cover with baking parchment to prevent a brown skin forming on the pudding. Bake in the preheated oven for about 2–2½ hours until creamy and thick.

Remove from the oven and take out and discard the lemon zest and vanilla pod. Spoon the pudding into 4 large ramekins and let cool until lukewarm.

Cut the pineapple and bananas into evenly-sized chunks and thread onto the satay sticks. Sift icing sugar onto the skewered fruit and caramelize under a hot grill or with a cook's blowtorch.

Dust the puddings with a thick layer of icing sugar and caster sugar and caramelize as before. Let cool until set, then serve the puddings with the caramelized fruit skewers.

crusted lime polenta cake

This is a beautiful moist pudding with a delicious tangy lime kick. Serve this with ice cream rather than mascarpone, if you prefer – coconut ice cream would make a perfect partner for the lime.

225 g unsalted butter

225 g caster sugar

3 eggs, beaten

½ teaspoon vanilla essence

225 g ground almonds

grated zest and juice of 3 limes

115 g polenta flour

1 teaspoon baking powder

a pinch of salt

mascarpone cheese, to serve

LIME CRUST

freshly squeezed juice of 2 limes

3 tablespoons caster sugar

a loose-based cake tin, 25 cm diameter, buttered and floured

SERVES 8–10

Preheat the oven to 170°C (325°F) Gas 3. Put the butter and sugar into a large mixing bowl and beat with an electric whisk until pale and light. Gradually add the eggs, beating all the time. Using a large metal spoon, stir in the vanilla essence and ground almonds, then fold in the lime zest and juice, polenta flour, baking powder and salt.

Spoon into the prepared cake tin. Bake for about 1¼ hours or until just set and golden brown.

Meanwhile, to make the lime crust, put the lime juice and sugar into a bowl and mix well.

When the cake is cooked, prick well with a skewer all over the surface and pour over the lime crust mix. Let cool for 15 minutes in the tin.

Remove the cake from the tin and serve still warm or let cool completely before slicing. Serve with mascarpone.

basics

For a really good pizza dough, try to use the superfine durum wheat '00' flour, which you can buy in Italian stores and large supermarkets. Otherwise, choose a strong white bread flour. Some cooks add flavourings such as chopped herbs or grated cheese to the dough, but if you keep it simple the toppings can take centre stage.

basic pizza dough

250 g tipo '00' or strong white bread flour, plus extra for sprinkling

½ teaspoon table salt

7 g sachet easy-blend dried yeast

2 tablespoons olive oil

125 ml tepid water

SERVES 4

Put the flour, salt and yeast in a large bowl and mix. Make a well in the centre. Add the oil and water to the well and gradually work in the flour to make a soft dough. Sprinkle over a little flour if the mixture feels too sticky, but make sure it is not too dry: the dough should be pliable and smooth.

Transfer the dough to a lightly floured surface. Knead for 10 minutes, sprinkling with flour when needed, until the dough is smooth and stretchy.

Rub some oil over the surface of the dough and return the dough to the bowl. Cover with a clean tea towel and leave for about 1 hour, until the dough has doubled in size.

Remove the dough to a lightly floured surface and knead for 2 minutes, until the excess air is knocked out. Roll out the dough according to the recipe you are following.

polenta dough

To make a polenta base, use 50 g fine polenta or cornmeal mixed with 200 g tipo '00' flour or strong white bread flour.

classic tomato sauce

1 tablespoon
olive oil

1 shallot, finely
chopped

2 garlic cloves,
finely chopped

400 g canned
whole plum
tomatoes

a sprig of fresh
rosemary or
thyme, or a pinch
of dried oregano

a pinch of sugar

sea salt and freshly
ground black
pepper

SERVES 4

Heat the oil in a small saucepan, add the shallot and garlic and cook for 3–4 minutes until softened. Add the tomatoes, breaking them up briefly with a wooden spoon. Add the herbs, sugar, and salt and pepper to taste.

Bring to the boil and part cover with a lid. Reduce the heat and simmer very gently for 30–60 minutes, stirring from time to time and breaking the tomatoes down with the back of the spoon, until the sauce turns a dark red and droplets of oil appear on the surface.

Discard any woody herb sprigs. Taste and adjust the seasoning, then let cool slightly before using.

This simple sauce is perfect as a basic topping for almost any pizza or with pasta. Choose cans of whole plum tomatoes rather than the chopped sort, which can have a bitter edge. Cook the sauce for at least 30 minutes to give it time to develop some richness.

fiery tomato sauce

500 g carton creamed
tomatoes or passata

2 tablespoons olive oil

2 garlic cloves, finely chopped

6 basil leaves, torn

a pinch of crushed
dried chillies

¼ teaspoon sugar

sea salt and freshly ground
black pepper

SERVES 4–6

The crushed dried chillies add an extra kick to this smooth, satiny sauce. Use it as an alternative to the Classic Tomato Sauce in any of the pizza recipes in this book. The basil is not essential, but is worth adding if you have some to hand.

Put the tomatoes, oil, garlic, basil, chillies and sugar in a saucepan with salt and pepper to taste.

Bring to the boil and part cover with a lid. Reduce the heat and simmer very gently, stirring from time to time, for 30–60 minutes, until the sauce turns a dark red and droplets of oil appear on the surface.

Taste and adjust the seasoning, if necessary, cover with the lid and let cool slightly before using.

tomato sauce with double basil

In summer, make this with fresh, ripe tomatoes. Otherwise, use canned Italian plum tomatoes. The basil is added in two stages; first for depth of flavour, then at the end for a burst of fresh fragrance. Serve with pasta and grated Parmesan.

3 tablespoons olive oil

2 garlic cloves, finely chopped

1 shallot, finely chopped

25 g basil leaves

500 g ripe tomatoes, coarsely chopped, or 400 g canned plum tomatoes

a pinch of sugar

sea salt and freshly ground black pepper

SERVES 4

Heat the oil in a saucepan and add the garlic, shallot and half the basil. Cook for 3–4 minutes until the shallot is golden.

Add the tomatoes and cook, stirring, for 10 minutes, until thickened and pulpy. Add the sugar, 100 ml water and salt and pepper to taste.

Bring to the boil, part cover with a lid and simmer very gently for 1 hour until dark red and thickened, with droplets of oil on the surface.

Tear the remaining basil into the tomato sauce just before serving.

crispy crumbs

These make a great addition to any tomato-based pasta dish.

Heat a couple of tablespoons of olive oil in a frying pan and add a good handful or two of fresh white breadcrumbs. Cook over a high heat, stirring until golden brown. The smaller crumbs will go to the bottom of the pan and char a little, but that's good. Serve straight from the pan, sprinkled on top of the pasta, while the crumbs are still hot and sizzling.

classic basil pesto

50 g basil leaves

2 tablespoons pine nuts

2 garlic cloves

2 tablespoons olive oil

50 g butter, softened

50 g freshly grated Parmesan cheese

freshly ground black pepper

SERVES 4

Melt over hot pasta or rice dishes, or serve as an accompaniment to grilled vegetables. Toast the pine nuts in a dry frying pan until golden for a variation of this vibrant basil sauce.

Put the basil, pine nuts and garlic into a food processor and process until finely chopped. Add the oil, butter, Parmesan and freshly ground black pepper to taste. Process briefly until blended.

It is preferable to use home-made stock when making risotto or soup as it gives the best flavour. Make a stock with whatever fresh vegetables are available, then refrigerate or freeze until needed.

vegetable stock

40 g unsalted butter

1 tablespoon olive oil

3 garlic cloves, crushed

1 large onion, chopped

4 leeks, chopped

2 carrots, chopped

2 celery sticks, chopped

1 fennel bulb, chopped

a handful of fresh flat leaf parsley, chopped

4 fresh or 2 dried bay leaves

2 sprigs of thyme

MAKES ABOUT 1 LITRE

Melt the butter and oil in a large, heavy-based saucepan. Add the garlic, fry for 2 minutes, then add the remaining ingredients. Cook, stirring constantly, until softened but not browned.

Add 3 litres water and bring to the boil. Reduce the heat, cover and simmer for 1½ hours. Let cool.

Return the pan to the heat and simmer for 15 minutes. Strain the stock and return to the pan. Discard the solids. Boil rapidly until reduced by half, then use as needed or let cool and keep in the fridge for up to 3 days.

dijon dressing

A simple all-purpose dressing for salads. You can adjust this as much as you like. Try wholegrain mustard in place of smooth, and experiment with different vinegars – sherry, cider, red wine or even Japanese rice vinegar.

1 tablespoon smooth Dijon mustard

1 tablespoon white wine vinegar

4 tablespoons extra virgin olive oil

1 garlic clove, crushed

sea salt and freshly ground black pepper

SERVES 4

Put the mustard, vinegar, oil and garlic in a bowl and mix with a fork or small metal whisk.

Add enough water for the consistency you want – about 1–2 tablespoons – and salt and black pepper to taste.

Any leftover dressing can be stored in a screw-top jar in the refrigerator.

fresh red pepper jam

Superb with pasta or on top of toasted bread with shavings of cheese.

2 tablespoons
olive oil

2 red peppers,
halved, deseeded
and finely sliced

2 yellow peppers,
halved, deseeded
and finely sliced

2 orange peppers,
halved, deseeded
and finely sliced

1 red chilli, halved,
deseeded and
finely sliced
diagonally

2 garlic cloves,
peeled

1 tablespoon sugar

1 lemon, halved

sea salt and freshly
ground black
pepper

SERVES 4

Heat the oil in a large saucepan. Add the peppers, chilli, garlic and sugar. Squeeze the lemon juice into the pan, then add the squeezed halves. Stir.

Put a piece of wet, crumpled greaseproof paper on top of the mixture in the pan and cover with a lid. Cook gently over low heat for 35–40 minutes until the peppers are meltingly soft. Remove the paper from the pan and increase the heat for about 3–4 minutes to reduce the liquid. Add salt and pepper to taste and remove from the heat. When cool, transfer to sterilized jars. Keep refrigerated and use within 1–2 weeks.

index

credits

Tessa Bramley
Braised root vegetables
Curried parsnips and squash
Potato, sage and apple gratin
Raspberry and passionfruit pavlova
Rhubarb crumble with ginger and vanilla
Rice pudding with caramelized pineapple and banana
Vegetable tian with mozarella and oregano

Ursula Ferrigno
Artichoke risotto
Courgette and ricotta risotto
Pumpkin risotto
Rice balls
Tomato risotto
Vegetable stock

Silvana Franco
Basic pizza dough
Broccoli and pine nut pesto
Charred vegetable polenta pizza
Classic sauces: classic basil pesto, classic tomato, fiery tomato, tomato with double basil
Fiorentina
Molten cheese and gremolata calzone
Pasta e fagioli soup
Pasta with roasted pumpkin and sage, lemon and mozarella butter
Three cheese baked penne

Alastair Hendy
Autumn lasagne with soft goats' cheese
Baby mushroom salad with golden beetroot and ginger
Peppered button mushrooms on buttery toast
Pesto-stuffed portobello mushrooms
Pink oyster and shiitake mushrooms with crisp tofu
Wild mushroom and potato pasties

Louise Pickford
Barbecued artichokes with chilli lime mayonnaise
Berries with honeyed yogurt
Blackberry buttermilk pancakes with apple butter
Cinnamon-soaked granola
Creamy eggs with goats' cheese
Honey-roasted peaches
Mixed mushroom frittata
Mushroom burgers with shallot jam
Omelette *fines herbes*
Onion, thyme and goats' cheese tarts
Pasta, squash and feta salad
Summer leaf and herb salad
Warm blueberry and almond muffins

Fiona Smith
Fonduta
Roasted red pepper cheese fondue
Vacherin fondue with caramelized shallots

Fran Warde
Artichoke and cheese tart
Asparagus and roasted peppers
Avocado and chickpea salad
Baked fennel with shallots and spicy dressing
Bean and mint salad
Beetroot, goats' cheese and pine nut salad with melba toast
Butternut and cashew nut soup
Carrot and spinach butter mash
Chickpea and vegetable curry
Chickpea, tomato and pepper salad
Courgette and cheddar on toast
Crusted golden rice bake
Curried lentils and spinach
Focaccia
French toast and fried tomatoes
Garlic bread
Ginger asparagus with cashews
Green bean and herb soup
Haricot bean and tomato salad

Honey and almond panna cotta
Hoummus and salad in Turkish flatbread
Mozzarella-baked tomatoes
Mozzarella cheese with fennel and new potatoes
Mushroom risotto
Nectarine tart
Noodle mountain
Panzanella
Poached mushrooms with egg noodles
Ricepaper parcels with dipping soy
Rich root soup with tarragon drizzle
Roast pumpkin, red onions, baby potatoes and fennel with chickpeas in tomato sauce
Sodabread
Spinach and ricotta filo pastries
Stuffed peppers
Summer beans and couscous salad
Tiramisu
Toasted Turkish bread
Vegetable couscous
Vegetable noodle stir-fry
Warm chocolate and coffee pudding
Warm Mediterranean Puy lentil salad
Watercress soup
White and green bean salad

Lesley Waters
Aubergine steaks with feta salad
Crusted lime polenta cake
Dijon dressing
Fresh red pepper jam
Herby potato rösti
Honey teriyaki vegetables
New potato salad with gazpacho dressing
Pan-grilled bruschetta with onion marmalade and goats' cheese
Rich red pepper and bean soup
Rocket eggs with salsa verde
Root vegetable chunky chips with coriander mayo

Simple spaghetti with capers and olives
Tomato tapenade salad
Vegetable goulash
Wild mushroom soup with sour cream and chives

Photographs

Peter Cassidy
Endpapers, pages 1, 2, 3, 4–5, 51, 55, 60–61, 71, 72, 87, 90–91, 97, 102, 105, 110, 114, 147, 200, 204, 222, 224–225, 234, 235

Christine Hanscomb
Pages 206–207, 210, 218

William Lingwood
Pages 62–63, 76–77, 79, 80, 82–83, 118–119, 121, 122–123, 124, 136–137, 138–139, 142–143, 144, 226–227, 228–229, 230–231

Jason Lowe
Pages 158–159, 161, 162, 168–169, 170, 173, 232–233

Craig Robertson
Pages 188–189, 192–193, 195, 198–199, 202–203, 221

Debi Treloar
Pages 6, 20, 24–25, 27, 31, 32, 35, 36, 39, 40, 43, 44, 48, 52, 64, 67, 68, 74, 93, 101, 109 113, 117, 128, 132, 135, 151, 152, 155, 156, 165, 166, 177, 178, 181, 182, 185, 186, 191, 196, 209, 213, 214, 217

Ian Wallace
Pages 8–9, 11, 12, 15, 16, 19, 23, 56, 59, 84, 88, 98, 106, 127

Simon Walton
Pages 28, 47, 94, 131, 140, 148

Philip Webb
Pages 174–175